D1716110

Ancient EGYPT

THE LAND OF PYRAMIDS AND PHARAOHS

By Nicole Horning

Portions of this book originally appeared in *Ancient Egypt* by Don Nardo.

LUCENT
PRESS

Published in 2018 by
Lucent Press, an Imprint of Greenhaven Publishing, LLC
353 3rd Avenue
Suite 255
New York, NY 10010

Designer: Seth Hughes
Editor: Siyavush Saidian

Library of Congress Cataloging-in-Publication Data

Names: Horning, Nicole, author.
Title: Ancient Egypt : the land of pyramids and pharaohs / Nicole Horning.
Other titles: World history series.
Description: New York : Lucent Press, 2018. | Series: World history |
  Includes bibliographical references and index.
Identifiers: LCCN 2017032412 | ISBN 9781534562462 (library bound book)| ISBN 9781534563063
(paperback)
Subjects: LCSH: Egypt–History–To 332 B.C.–Juvenile literature. |
  Egypt–Civilization–Juvenile literature.
Classification: LCC DT83 .H56 2018 | DDC 932/.01–dc23
LC record available at https://lccn.loc.gov/2017032412
Printed in the United States of America

CPSIA compliance information: Batch #CW18KL: For further information contact Greenhaven Publishing LLC, New York, New York at 1-844-317-7404.

Contents

Foreword

History books are often filled with names and dates—words and numbers for students to memorize for a test and forget once they move on to another class. However, what history books should be filled with are great stories, because the history of our world is filled with great stories. Love, death, violence, heroism, and betrayal are not just themes found in novels and movie scripts. They are often the driving forces behind major historical events.

When told in a compelling way, fact is often far more interesting—and sometimes far more unbelievable—than fiction. World history is filled with more drama than the best television shows, and all of it really happened. As readers discover the incredible truth behind the triumphs and tragedies that have impacted the world since ancient times, they also come to understand that everything is connected. Historical events do not exist in a vacuum. The stories that shaped world history continue to shape the present and will undoubtedly shape the future.

The titles in this series aim to provide readers with a comprehensive understanding of pivotal events in world history. They are written with a focus on providing readers with multiple perspectives to help them develop an appreciation for the complexity of the study of history. There is no set lens through which history must be viewed, and these titles encourage readers to analyze different viewpoints to understand why a historical figure acted the way they did or why a contemporary scholar wrote what they did about a historical event. In this way, readers are able to sharpen their critical-thinking skills and apply those skills in their history classes. Readers are aided in this pursuit by formally documented quotations and annotated bibliographies, which encourage further research and debate.

Many of these quotations come from carefully selected primary sources, including diaries, public records, and contemporary research and writings. These valuable primary sources help readers hear the voices of those who directly experienced historical events, as well as the voices of biographers and historians who provide a unique perspective on familiar topics. Their voices all help history come alive in a vibrant way.

As students read the titles in this series, they are provided with clear context in the form of maps, timelines, and informative text. These elements give them the basic facts they need to fully appreciate the high drama that is history.

The study of history is difficult at times—not because of all the information that needs to be memorized, but because of the challenging questions it asks us. How could something as horrible as the Holocaust happen? Why would religious leaders use torture during the Inquisition? Why does ISIS have so many followers? The information presented in each title gives readers the tools they need to confront these questions and participate in the debates they inspire.

As we pore over the stories of events and eras that changed the world, we come to understand a simple truth: No one can escape being a part of history. We are not bystanders; we are active participants in the stories that are being created now and will be written about in history books decades and even centuries from now. The titles in this series help readers gain a deeper appreciation for history and a stronger understanding of the connection between the stories of the past and the stories they are part of right now.

SETTING THE SCENE: A TIMELINE

Pharaoh Narmer unites Upper and Lower Egypt into one unified nation-state.

Pharaoh Ahmose rules Egypt, bringing stability to the country.

Powerful female pharaoh Hatshepsut reigns in Egypt.

The New Kingdom in Egypt is founded, encompassing the 18th, 19th, and 20th ruling dynasties.

The Old Kingdom in Egypt, which is famous for the construction of pyramids, is founded.

1274 BC ········· 1174 BC ·········· 32 BC ·········· 1922 ········· 2017

Cleopatra VII, the last pharaoh of Egypt, dies.

Egypt engages in battle against the Sea Peoples; Pharaoh Ramses III leads his people to victory.

Archaeologists discover a 3,700-year-old pyramid in Egypt.

The Battle of Kadesh is fought; each side claims victory despite there being no clear winner.

Archaeologist Howard Carter discovers the tomb of King Tutankhamun.

OPPOSING VIEWPOINTS OF ANCIENT EGYPT

Egypt has been a subject of fascination for many throughout history, and researchers have studied artifacts for many years to learn what they can about their customs and ways of life. While ancient Egypt is currently a popular topic in movies and books, interest in ancient Egyptian history goes back as far as the first century BC. However, with this early fascination also came two different views of the Egyptians' way of life. One view was from foreign visitors, some of whom traveled to Egypt and later wrote about it. Among them were the Greek historians Herodotus and Diodorus Siculus, the Greek biographer Plutarch, and various Roman and European writers.

Suffering Under Foreign Rule

Due to differences in cultures and visitors not speaking the Egyptian language, they did not understand many of Egypt's customs and traditions. The result was a vision of Egypt as a land of mystery. Herodotus enjoyed his stay in the country and was also impressed by the giant pyramids and other architectural wonders. The land had "more monuments which [are difficult to describe] than anywhere else in the world," he stated. However, Herodotus was also quick to point out that

in keeping with the odd climate which prevails there and the fact that their river behaves differently than any other river, almost all Egyptian customs and practices are the opposite of those of everywhere else. For instance, women go out to the town square and retail goods, while men stay at home and do the weaving; and whereas everyone else weaves by pushing the weft upwards, the Egyptians push it downwards. Or again, men carry loads on their heads while women do so on their shoulders … animals and humans live together in Egypt. Other people live off barley and ordinary wheat, but Egyptians regard it as demeaning to make those grains one's staple diet ... [In addition] they are exceedingly religious, more so than any other people in the world.[1]

While Herodotus was critical of Egypt and took note of the cultural differences, he also noticed that they had been under foreign rule for too long and suffering for it. Many years before his trip to Egypt, the Assyrians, a warlike people who inhabited Mesopotamia (what is now Iraq), had invaded and conquered the country. During Herodotus's time, that land was controlled by the Persians (from Iran), who had invaded in 525 BC. Later, in the fourth century BC, the Macedonian Greek conqueror Alexander the Great took charge of Egypt. After his death, one of his generals—Ptolemy—declared himself pharaoh and established a Greek dynasty that ruled the country for three centuries. Later, Rome absorbed Egypt after defeating the last of the Ptolemies, Cleopatra VII, in 31 BC. Later still, following Rome's fall, other foreigners, including Arabs and Turks, ruled Egypt well into modern times.

This frequent change of foreign rulers and centuries of defeat created a poor reputation of Egypt among other nations. They began to view Egypt not as the great power it was, but as weak. In Plutarch's essay about Egypt, *Isis and Osiris*, he suggested that this was partly the fault of one of the ancient pharaohs. The pharaohs had, in his eyes, "planted among them an everlasting superstition, a ground for unceasing quarreling [among themselves] ... As a result of this, they became involved in war and inflicted much harm upon each other. And later, they were brought to order through the [intervention of] the Romans."[2]

Herodotus, who is depicted in this bust, was fascinated by ancient Egypt. However, he was also critical of their way of life in his book, Histories.

Removing the Mystery

Recent research takes into account the huge ruins dotting the country's landscape that have fascinated many around the world. Modern researchers, such as archaeologists, historians, and other scholars, do not dismiss these artifacts as too ancient and mysterious to understand. Instead, they closely examine them and attempt to understand their meaning and who their builders really were. From this viewpoint, the years Egypt suffered under foreign rule has nothing to do with their qualities as a people. Nor does it detract from the greatness and important legacy of the civilization their ancestors had created long before the Assyrians, Persians, Greeks, Romans, or Turks ruled.

Researchers try not to become distracted by the biased, distorted viewpoints that occur in the literature from the past. Rather, archaeologists and historians uncover and analyze what they can because archaeological remains, such as tombs, grave items, personal articles, and other artifacts, as well as ruined buildings, contain a wealth of information about the people who created them. Inscriptions that have been found in archaeological sites describe prayers, wars, battles, and more, and they tell the stories of ancient Egypt. The ancient Egyptians may have lived thousands of

Although the ruins in Egypt are thousands of years old, they still fascinate many around the world and still have many mysteries left to uncover.

years ago, but these stories and personal artifacts along with the buildings they created still have the power to capture the imagination.

The historical artifacts and inscriptions that have been found in the pyramids—and the pyramids themselves—allow researchers to portray ancient Egypt in a fairer, more complete, and accurate way than other literature of the time. While the artifacts and pyramids they created are fascinating on their own, the information gathered from these finds indicates that ancient Egyptians were not living unnaturally, as older literature may have portrayed. Instead, research has shown a culture that was full of proud, resourceful, hard working, and accomplished people who created the world's powerful first nation-state. The Egyptians created enormous pyramids and temples along the Nile, which is one of the world's longest rivers. Thousands of years later, these pyramids still have mysteries and artifacts left to find, and these objects are the center of much curiosity. While the Egyptians did create a great empire that fascinates to this day, the fact remains that for many years, they were under foreign rule. This partially caused the great pyramids to fall to ruin.

The interesting stories of the Egyptians that have inspired many books and movies were dormant for many years, waiting to be told. Once archaeologists began digging, their stories and culture were able to be revealed and ancient artifacts shown to the world on tours such as the *National Geographic* Exhibitions. According to the late historian Lionel Casson, archaeologists "stripped much of the mystery from ancient Egypt ... Its people and culture now stand revealed in their proper light as one of the great civilizations the world has known."[3]

CHAPTER ONE

EGYPT'S BEGINNINGS

The first-known nation-state was in the Nile Valley in around 3000 BC. This nation-state arose from the unification of Upper and Lower Egypt. The Nile Delta separated the two regions, with Upper Egypt being everything south of the Nile Delta and Lower Egypt being everything north of the Nile Delta. Because Upper Egypt actually looks lower on a map than Lower Egypt, many have questioned why they were named this way. Historians determined, however, that because the Nile River actually flows from south to north, the ancient Egyptians based their understanding of geography on that flow, which led to the reversal. Long before there was a ruler on a throne, evidence discovered by archaeologists indicates there were smaller villages that eventually formed the upper and lower kingdoms. Earlier still, evidence has been uncovered of groups of people living in the Nile Valley.

Predynastic Culture

The first leader of Egypt established a dynasty, or family line of rulers. This dynasty was the first of many to follow in Egypt. Researchers sometimes use the term Predynastic to describe Egypt and its history before the rise of the nation-state and its kingship. Specifically, the time period known as Predynastic lasted from around 5000 to 3100 BC. The peoples that had settled in this area were descendants of inhabitants from northeast Africa who had spread over the area during the Paleolithic period. During this timeframe, there were a number of key events that ultimately led to the emergence of the Egyptian state.

Research indicates that early humans passed through the Nile Valley as far back as 1.8 million years ago, during the Stone Age. Later, between 50,000 and 100,000 years ago, groups of modern humans settled permanently in the Nile River valley. They were hunter-gatherers, which means that they supported themselves by hunting, fishing, and gathering berries, roots, and wild plants.

As late as 6000 BC, Egypt was still inhabited by hunter-gatherers. However, around 5000 BC, this began to change, and agriculture started to be introduced on small scales in local cultures. Evidence shows that these early cultures came south through Egypt and into the Sudan. Additionally, many of the plants that were grown were native to the Middle East, which indicates they may have come from that region. This marked the beginning of the country's crucial Predynastic period.

The first known small-scale farming in Egypt was practiced along the shores of Lake Faiyum, which was located a few miles southwest of the Nile Delta. The locals, making up what scholars call Faiyumian culture, grew barley, emmer wheat, and flax. They also fished and raised livestock, including pigs, sheep, and cattle. As the Predynastic Period progressed, knowledge of farming and raising livestock steadily spread through the Nile's marshlands.

Lakes, such as the one shown here in the Faiyum Oasis, were important to early Egyptians.

HAPY HYMNAL

The Nile River was important to the Egyptians and their existence. They were aware that the annual floods were important to their existence, and they created a hymn (or religious song) dedicated to Hapy. Hapy was a spirit that brought abundance and fertility, and these topics were the focus of their hymn to the Nile:

> May your countenance [face] shine on us, Hapy, god of the
> moving river,
>> who comes forth from earth
>>> returning to save the Black Land [Egypt].
> His features are hidden, dark in the daylight,
>> yet the faithful find him fit subject for song.
> He waters the landscape the Sun god has formed,
>> giving life to every small creature ...
>
> Food bringer, rich with provisions,
>> himself the author of all his good things,
> Awe-striking master, yet sweet the aromas rising about him,
>> and, how he satisfies when he returns!—
> Transforming the dust to pastures for cattle ...
>
> Filling the storerooms, heaping the grainsheds,
>> giving his gifts to the poor.[1]

1. Quoted in John L. Foster, trans., *Ancient Egyptian Literature.* Austin, TX: University of Texas Press, 2001, pp. 111–113.

River-Based Agriculture

The landscape is important to any culture and has a large influence on how that culture develops. This was especially true for the Egyptians. At some unknown date, but at least by 4000 BC, Egyptian farmers learned to water their fields by taking advantage of the Nile's yearly floods. From July through September, the river overflowed its banks; during these floods, the waters laid down a fresh layer of rich soil and provided sufficient moisture to grow enormous amounts of crops. Using the Nile's floods made it possible to practice agriculture on a much larger scale than before and stimulated both population increases and the development of more complex social customs.

The Nile River, shown here, is incredibly important to the Egyptians and their culture.

This marked the emergence of the Egyptian civilization that Herodotus witnessed more than three millennia later. In his book, *Histories*, he revealed how important the Nile River was to the Egyptian civilization: "It is clear to any intelligent observer, even if he has no previous information on the subject, that the Egypt to which we sail nowadays is, as it were, the gift of the river and has come only recently into the possession of its inhabitants."[4]

The manner in which the early Egyptians used the Nile and made it the center of their lives was based in large part on the physical realities of the river and the lands surrounding it. One of the world's longest rivers, the Nile rises in the highlands of east-central Africa and flows more than 4,132 miles (6,649 km) northward to its delta, in northern Egypt, where it empties into the Mediterranean Sea. Only a narrow band of territory bordering the river was fertile and capable of supporting large numbers of people. Most of the rest of Egypt consisted of dry desert wastelands difficult for humans to live on. Therefore, the well-watered strip along the riverbanks—measuring a mere 4 to 13 miles (6.4 to 21 km) wide in most places—was where the vast majority of Egyptians lived. People mostly used the Nile's waters for irrigating crops, drinking, and bathing. However, they also transformed those waters into a natural highway by launching small boats fashioned from bundles of papyrus, a plant that grew along the riverbanks. In time, the Egyptians also learned to make a kind of paper from papyrus, which became one of the country's chief economic exports.

The large, dependable food source provided by river-based agriculture also stimulated the growth of small villages throughout the fertile portions of the Nile Valley, as farmers tended to band together for mutual aid and protection. Such cooperation among the villagers naturally stimulated the development of new ideas and practices. Among these were the production of new and better tools, utensils, and vessels (including bowls, cups, and storage containers) made of stone, and, eventually, pottery. As local populations grew, some of the small villages inevitably became large ones.

Communities Form

Sometime in the fourth millennium BC, groups of neighboring villages across Egypt started banding together to form what they called sepats. A single sepat typically included a collection of several villages that were close together and the farmlands that supported those towns. The term nome was later coined by the Greeks to describe a sort of township or small province consisting of several villages and their surrounding farmlands. Each nome was overseen by a local leader, often called the nomarch. Historians and researchers do not know specifically why and how the nomes originally formed and how they were administered.

What is more certain is that the Egyptian nomes eventually numbered 42. They came to be divided into 2 large groups—1 in Lower Egypt, containing 20 nomes, the other in Upper Egypt, containing 22 nomes. In the mid-fourth millennium BC, each of the two collections of nomes came together into a political unit with a king. One of these kingdoms, the Red Land, was in the North. It encompassed the fertile delta and extended southward as far

THE FLOOD AND EGYPTIAN CALENDAR

The world of the ancient Egyptians was defined by two cycles. First was the rising and setting of the sun, which also symbolized creation in their religious beliefs, and second was the flooding of the Nile River, which was integral to their daily lives and food source. From this, they created a sophisticated calendar that dictated the planting and harvesting of crops.

The appearance of the star Sirius marked their New Year's Day, which they called Wep-Renpet, or the "Opening of the Year." Following this was

> the four months of Inundation (Shemu) ... each divided into three weeks of ten days each. The months during which the flood receded, fields were prepared, and seeds planted were known as Emergence (Peret). Four months later came the Harvest (Akhet), followed again by Inundation. Five "epagomenal" days were inserted at the end of the year in order to bring it up to 365 days. However, a solar year is 365 and 1/4 days long, so over the centuries the actual year fell out of sync with the civil calendar and the official seasons ceased to correspond with the agricultural cycle. Aided by their skill in astronomy and by their careful record-keeping, the Egyptians were able to correct for this discrepancy and kept a second calendar more closely tied to the changing seasons.[1]

1. Zahi Hawass, *Tutankhamun and the Golden Age of the Pharaohs*. Washington, DC: National Geographic, 2011, p. 54.

as Atfih. The capital of the Red Land was Pe (later called Buto), in the delta. The other early kingdom was the White Land, occupying the southern part of Egypt. Its capital was Nekhen (later Hierakonpolis), lying on the Nile south of Atfih.

Partly because they did not keep written historical records, not a lot is known about these realms and their leaders. Also obscure are the details of a major event that may have occurred during the first two centuries of their existence.

One controversial theory is the Dynastic Race theory of archaeologist Sir William Matthew Flinders Petrie. His theory was that another group of foreigners from Mesopotamia or elsewhere in the Near East entered Egypt. These outsiders supposedly brought with them new ideas and customs. Among them were distinctive burial customs (placing the bodies of kings and other nobles in brick tombs rather than shallow sand pits, as had been the custom in the past); advanced building techniques that made large-scale architecture possible; and the concept of writing using a combination of symbols and pictures.

The majority of scholars and historians are not convinced of this theory, however. They say that the indigenous Egyptians were more than capable of developing these innovations on their own. Also, many critics argue, though the basic concept of writing was the same in Egypt and Mesopotamia, the actual symbols of the two systems were different. The Egyptian practice of writing using symbols, called hieroglyphics, bears little resemblance to cuneiform, the series of wedge-shaped symbols used in ancient Mesopotamia. In addition, no physical evidence of a mass

invasion of Egypt in this period has ever been found. University of Manchester scholar Rosalie David suggested that "trade, rather than mass invasion or armed conflict, may have introduced these innovations into Egypt."[5]

In whatever manner the Egyptians acquired the idea of brick tombs and the techniques needed to build them, these innovations would, in the course of only a few generations, have a profound effect on Egyptian culture. They gave Egyptian leaders the ability to erect large monuments and even entire cities of brick. For the large workforces required to make these structures a reality, they could draw on thousands of ordinary Egyptians.

Scholars do not believe Mesopotamians introduced writing symbols to the early Egyptians. Cuneiform (left), uses wedge-shaped symbols, whereas hieroglyphics (right) uses more distinct pictures.

Unification of the Red and White Lands

Even if a group of conquerors from the Middle East did enter Egypt in the last few centuries of the Predynastic Period, these outsiders were rapidly absorbed into the country's population and culture. Except for trade, during the next several centuries, Egypt remained more or less isolated from the rest of the Near East. The Egyptians instead focused their political and cultural energy inward into a growing rivalry between the Red and White lands. Whether or not these rivals ever waged full wars or battles against each other is not confirmed by historians. However, a small piece of visual evidence has been found. It consists of scenes carved into the head of a limestone mace (war club) belonging to Scorpion, the ruler of the White Land. Some of the carved figures have been identified as war captives, so it may be that this king attempted to conquer the northern kingdom. If so, he failed.

However, one of his immediate successors was more successful. In about 3100 BC, another southern ruler, Narmer (also called Menes), united Upper and Lower Egypt into a single, powerful nation-state. Among the surviving artifacts relating to Narmer is a flat stone plate found at Hierakonpolis in 1897. The Narmer Palette, as historians have named it, is about 25 inches (64 cm) high and has well preserved carvings on both sides. On one side, Narmer wears the distinctive crown of the White Land, while on the other side, he wears the crown of the Red Land. In his book *Egypt, Greece, and Rome: Civilizations of the Ancient Mediterranean*, historian Charles Freeman described the Narmer Palette:

> *Quite apart from its historical importance, the palette shows that many conventions of Egyptian art are already in place. Status is represented by the comparative size of the figures. Narmer is the largest figure throughout. In one scene an official is shown as smaller than Narmer but still much larger than the accompanying standard-bearers. The artist is not concerned so much with providing a proper representation as with passing on detail, even if this means distorting normal perspectives. The face of the king, for instance, is shown in profile, but his eye is shown in full and the shoulders are viewed from the front.*[6]

As the first king of Egypt's first dynasty, Narmer was later recognized as the country's first pharaoh. The word pharaoh is an ancient Greek version of the Egyptian term *per-aa*, meaning "great house." It originally referred to the royal palace. The Egyptians themselves did not begin to use it to describe their kings until late in the New Kingdom. However, modern studies of ancient Egypt use the term pharaoh to describe all Egyptian kings beginning with Narmer.

The Scorpion macehead, shown here, depicts the ruler of the White Land engaging in both irrigation projects and military action.

To demonstrate the importance of national unity, Narmer established a new capital city, Memphis, somewhat north of the boundary between the former rival kingdoms. The name Memphis, based on *Men-nefer*, meaning "established and beautiful," came later. In Narmer's time, the city was called Ineb-hedj, meaning "White Fortress," most likely taking its name from the whitewashed walls of the palace. There, the pharaoh established a central government for the new country. He chose a chief administrator, known as a vizier, a position that would remain intact and important throughout the rest of

Egyptian history. Other government officials were also put into place.

Not only did the traditional nomes remain intact, but the concept of the original two kingdoms was also retained, as all subsequent pharaohs called themselves kings of the "Two Lands." This was done to emphasize the importance of unity. Various official symbols were adopted to reflect this unity. For example, Narmer introduced a crown that combined the main features of the crowns worn by the rulers of the Red and White lands. This same crown was worn by almost every subsequent pharaoh.

The Narmer Palette depicts Narmer wearing the crown of the Red Land on one side (right) and the crown of the White Land (left) on the other.

The Kingship Emerges

Also firmly established in the early years of the first dynasty was the idea that Egypt's pharaohs were absolute monarchs whose word was law. They were seen not just as kings, but also as divine beings, earthly manifestations of some of the gods worshiped throughout the land. According to the emerging religious mythology surrounding the kingship, the pharaoh's connection with heavenly forces was necessary to help the country and its people maintain *ma'at*. This was the state of natural and divine order and harmony that made it possible for the gods and human civilization to emerge from a state of chaos. As scholar David P. Silverman explained,

RELIGION AS A WAY OF LIFE

Religion was not merely a belief system to the ancient Egyptians—it was a way of life. At some point, the Egyptians began to question how the world was created and who controlled the things that dominated their daily lives. From this point, creation myths began and agriculture and the Nile were the basis for the religious system:

> The yearly cycle of the Inundation gave rise to the myth of creation, in which a primordial mound rose from limitless darkness and water, providing a platform on which the creator god could stand to work his magic. The sun, with its regular and unchanging cycle, was the most prominent feature of the natural world. It rose each day, bringing light and life to the earth, and disappeared every night, leaving the world in darkness. It was the visible expression of the daily cycle of creation.[1]

By the time of the pharaohs, the Egyptian pantheon was composed of many gods and goddesses. These were represented in art as humans, animals, or a combination of the two. Each was linked to one or more towns and identified by specific characteristics. For example, the principal god of Memphis was Ptah, patron of artisans; he was worshiped there with his consort, Sekhmet, goddess of war, and their son, Nefertem. In Abydos, the chief god was Osiris, king of the dead, worshiped with his sister-wife Isis and their child Horus.

1. Zahi Hawass, *Tutankhamun and the Golden Age of the Pharaohs*. Washington, DC: National Geographic, 2011, pp. 79–80.

Without Pharaoh, the cosmos would be in disarray and the world would descend into chaos. The king was an active participant in the mythology associated with kingship, fulfilling on earth the role of the god Horus, son of Osiris [ruler of the Underworld] … The monarch was also regarded as the living descendant of the sun god. A pharaoh acquired this deified status upon his coronation.[7]

Besides acting as a divine figure for the nation, the pharaoh was also the supreme commander of the country's armies and led the troops on military campaigns. During the course of the first several dynasties, such large and lengthy battles were not common. This was mainly because Egypt was still largely isolated from the outside world and therefore had no major enemies. As time went on, this gave the Egyptians a somewhat distorted sense of self-importance. The common view was that their land rested at the center of the universe, and both the heavens and other human communities revolved around Egypt. Foreigners came to be seen as secondary, hostile, backward, evil, or cowardly—in general, they were treated as a potential threat to the righteous order. Encouraged by this arrogant attitude, most later military operations launched by the pharaohs were viewed not as wars, but as punishments designed to restore the natural order that the foreigners had temporarily upset.

Thus, as Egypt became unified and entered what scholars call the Early Dynastic Period (2925 to 2575 BC), encompassing the first two dynasties, it demonstrated some profound fundamental strengths: It had a plentiful food supply provided by the Nile's reliable annual floods; it had longstanding traditions of efficient political and administrative organization exemplified by the nomes and early kingdoms; and it had a strong kingship rooted in and supported by religious beliefs devoutly held by most of the people. These strengths would allow the world's first nation to endure and prosper for many centuries to come.

CHAPTER TWO

PYRAMID BUILDING

After Narmer unified Egypt, the next 24 centuries were mostly ruled by native-born pharaohs. Historians informally refer to this period as the pharaonic period, but formally, it is divided by seven time spans. The first time span, the Early Dynastic Period, was from about 2925 to 2575 BC, and it encompassed the first, second, and third dynasties. The first dynasty was ruled by a succession of nine rulers, including Narmer and his successor, Aha, while the second had seven rulers. The sacred burial site of most of these pharaohs is at Abydos, which is along the Nile River south of Memphis. A few of the remaining pharaohs during these early years were buried at Saqqara, which is a few miles from Memphis.

Following the Early Dynastic Period was the period known as the Old Kingdom, which spanned the fourth through the eighth dynasties and the years from 2575 to 2130 BC. According to archaeological evidence from this time, the pharaohs were absolute rulers and their people looked on them as living gods. Some of the evidence of these pharaohs' power comes from the epic monuments that were created for their tombs dotting Egypt's landscape. The creation of these monuments still fascinates people across the world today. Created with millions of stone blocks and filled with well-preserved artifacts, such as statues large and small, model boats, paintings, and even coffins, these monuments have given this era its name—the "pyramid age"—and the kings their title—the "pyramid builders."

From Mastabas to Pyramids

Not all the Old Kingdom pharaohs had huge stone pyramids created. Quite a few of the pyramids built during this era were relatively small. These earlier tombs were called mastabas. The term came from a word meaning "bench" because they looked like the brick and wooden benches that many Egyptians

Many early pharaohs were buried at Abydos. Shown here are the ruins of Abydos (top) and the interior of the Abydos temple (bottom).

placed outside the front doors of their homes. A typical early mastaba had four outer walls and a flat top. The burial chamber was below ground and accessed by a vertical shaft or stairway. Above the burial chamber were one or more small rooms, sometimes including a chapel, in which certain items, including food, utensils, clothes, weapons, and even chariots and boats, were placed. It was believed that the deceased would need to use these objects in the afterlife.

The mastabas of the Old Kingdom were typically used for non-royal burials. Along the walls of the mastabas were paintings showing what it was thought that the deceased would be doing every day in the afterlife. The mastabas eventually even grew to include a false door so that the spirit of the deceased could leave.

A drawback of the mastabas was that they were initially composed of mud bricks, made by mixing moist mud with straw and allowing it to dry in the sun. The problem was that mud bricks deteriorated rapidly. Tombs and other structures made from these bricks steadily disintegrated and had to be repaired often.

Before Imhotep came up with a way to construct pyramids, the signature tomb in Egypt was a mastaba similar to this.

To address these problems, during the third dynasty, builders introduced changes in the construction of royal tombs. They began using stone, which is harder and more durable than mud bricks. They also made the mastabas larger, hoping that these structures would now be more permanent. At first, the tombs were rectangular with a flat top as they were earlier. However, an innovative architect named Imhotep, who served the pharaoh Djoser, came up with an ingenious idea. Instead of building a traditional mastaba, he stacked six stone mastabas on top of one another, each slightly smaller than the one below. The result was the first pyramid-tomb, which still exists in a fair state of preservation. Because the indentations of the rising mastabas created notches, or steps, it came to be called the step pyramid.

Other Old Kingdom pharaohs built step pyramids, among them Djoser's immediate successor, Sekhemkhet, and Sekhemkhet's successor, Khaba. It was not until the advent of the fourth dynasty that someone introduced the notion of filling in the notches on the

PYRAMID TEXTS

Among the artifacts found in the pyramids were Pyramid Texts. These Pyramid Texts were written on the walls in the sarcophagus chambers of the kings and were supposed to promote the resurrection of the deceased. The Pyramid Text of Pepi I was found in 1881 and included hundreds of short utterances such as the excerpt below:

> Pepi is one of the great group [of divinities] born [long ago] …
> Who are not brought before magistrates,
> Who are not made to suffer, who are not found guilty.
> Such is Pepi: he will not suffer …
> Pepi will not hunger,
> His nails will not grow long,
> No bone in him will be broken …
> Re [the sun god] will take Pepi by the hand …
> [The god] Geb will lift him up …
> > [The pharaoh] will be led by the hand to where a god may be [i.e., into the heavens].[1]

1. Quoted in Miriam Lichtheim, ed., *Ancient Egyptian Literature: A Book of Readings*, vol. 1. Berkeley, CA: University of California Press, 2006, p. 47.

sides of such a structure to produce a smooth-sided pyramid. The first pharaoh of the fourth dynasty, Sneferu, constructed three pyramids, making him the most constructive of the pyramid builders. One of these structures, at Meidum, began as a step pyramid. However, the pharaoh's builders later filled in the steps with extra stones at Sneferu's direction, converting it into a true pyramid. Sneferu's other pyramids all began as true pyramids.

After the mastabas and before what is known as the familiar standard pyramids, step pyramids such as Djoser's, shown here, were built.

Sneferu's Pyramids

Besides the pyramidal shape itself, Sneferu's pyramids had two important aspects that came to characterize those of his Old Kingdom successors, particularly his son, Khufu, and grandson, Khafre. First, each pyramid-tomb was not on its own. Rather, it was part of a larger complex of structures that included boat pits, a valley temple, and many small pyramids and tombs for some royal family members, some of them enclosed by a protective wall. For example, Sneferu's Meidum pyramid, the core of which survives, was surrounded by a wall. Both inside and outside the wall were traditional mastabas that were possibly intended for the pharaoh's relatives. Also inside the wall was a smaller pyramid, which historians think was used for religious rituals, and a small mortuary temple. Mortuary temples were built to honor the pharaohs and were staffed by priests who prayed and sacrificed to ensure that these rulers would make it to and thrive in the afterlife. Outside the enclosure wall in such pyramid complexes, an unroofed causeway led to another temple, generally referred to as a valley temple, the purpose of which is still debated by historians.

The other important aspect of the early pyramid-tombs of the Old Kingdom was their large size. Djoser's Step Pyramid, for example, had a base measuring 413 by 344 feet (126 by 105 m) and stood 204 feet (62 m) high. A number of the pyramids that followed during the fourth dynasty were much larger. The largest of these was Khufu's tomb, which was named Akhet-Khufu, or "Khufu's Horizon." Khufu's tomb is the largest pyramid that was ever built and originally towered to a height of 481 feet (147 m), measured 756 feet (230 m) on each side, and covered more than 13 acres (5 ha) of ground. Today, the structure stands 448 feet (136 m) high because the marble slabs that made up its original outer casing were stripped away over time. Creating the imposing pyramid took a lot of work—an estimated 2.3 million stone blocks that weigh between 2.5 and 15 tons (2.2 and 13.6 mt) each created the structure. Additionally, a block would have to be set every two-and-a-half minutes by the workers.

Inside the pyramid are three burial chambers. The first of these is underground, the second aboveground, which early explorers called the queen's chamber. However, recent research shows that it was never intended for a queen. Rather, it was meant to hold a statue of the king. The last chamber was the king's chamber, which was accessed by a 26 foot (8 m) high Grand Gallery. This gallery was even protected from grave robbers by sliding granite blocks.

Khafre's pyramid-tomb, also at Giza, was only slightly smaller than Khufu's, rising to a height of 471 feet (143 m). However, while Khafre's pyramid is smaller than Khufu's, it was built at a higher elevation and was also surrounded by an elaborate complex. "Outside the pyramid all the typical elements of a pharaonic mortuary temple are seen in one place for the first time: entrance hall, colonnaded courtyard, niches for royal statuary, storage chambers, and interior sanctuary. Later pyramids would be significantly smaller, with greater emphasis on these mortuary temples."[8] Beside these two giants is the pyramid-tomb of the fifth (or sixth, according to some traditions) pharaoh of the fourth dynasty, Menkaure. It stands 213 feet (65 m) high, and the bottom levels were made of granite, which was much more expensive and difficult to work with.

One reason for making these tombs so big was the importance of those who were laid to rest within them. Most Egyptians in the Old Kingdom saw the pharaoh not only as their leader, but also as a divine being. It seemed proper for someone of such great stature to have a tomb of equally grand proportions. Another benefit of making a pharaoh's tomb large was that, at least in theory, a more massive structure would be stronger and more difficult for tomb-robbers to penetrate. These efforts proved futile in the end, for virtually all the pyramid-tombs were robbed.

The pyramid of Khufu, which is sometimes called the Great Pyramid at Giza, is the largest pyramid ever built.

Building the Pyramids

Though the great size of the pyramids at Giza, Meidum, Dahshur, and other locations in Egypt continues to awe those who see them, how they were built is even more impressive. During the Old Kingdom, the Egyptians possessed primitive tools and construction methods. Because they lacked basic tools and techniques, such as pulleys and ropes, they had to rely almost entirely on levers and muscle power.

Naturally, it was not the pharaoh, nor his relatives, nor the country's nobles, priests, or various government officials who supplied this muscle power. Instead, hundreds, and at times thousands, of ordinary Egyptians toiled to raise the pyramids that came to be seen as the hallmarks of the Old Kingdom. Herodotus later claimed that Khufu was a tyrant who forced many of his subjects to work as slaves on massive building projects, including his tomb, which came to be called the Great Pyramid. Herodotus wrote that the pharaoh

> brought the country into all sorts of misery. He closed all the temples [so he could confiscate their wealth to help finance his pyramid, and] then, not content with excluding his subjects from the practice of their religion, compelled them without exception to labor as slaves for his own advantage. Some were forced to drag blocks of stone from the quarries ... to the Nile, where they were ferried across and taken over by others ... The work went

> on in three monthly shifts, a hundred thousand men in a shift. It took ten years of this oppressive slave labor to build the track along which the blocks were hauled ... To build the pyramid itself took twenty years.[9]

There may be some truth in this and other later stories claiming that Khufu was an authoritarian ruler. He and his immediate predecessors and successors were able to marshal the energies of an entire nation into a single project—one that ensured that one person, the king, would enjoy eternal life. This could only have been accomplished by a leader who was, as the late historian Chester G. Starr wrote, "the overpowering focus of earthly life." By the beginning of the fourth dynasty, Starr wrote, the government was a "royal absolutism" in which the pharaoh decided "all aspects of life, with the aid of a simple central administration."[10]

However, Herodotus and other writers of ancient Egypt lived more than 2,000 years after Khufu's time. Therefore, these stories would become increasingly exaggerated over time, and sometimes even blatantly wrong. Herodotus's mention of thousands of slaves working on the pyramids is one such example. Modern historians have revealed that these workers were not slaves, but free Egyptians. Most of them were rural farmers who took part in public building projects during their slow season, when the Nile's floodwaters were high and no planting or harvesting could be done. According to archaeologist Zahi Hawass, each gang, or group, that built Khufu's pyramid wrote their names in graffiti in the pyramid, and

> the names of the gangs of Khufu [were written] as "Friends of Khufu." Because they were the friends of Khufu proves that building the Pyramid was not really something that the Egyptians would push. It's like today. If you go to any village you will understand the system of ancient Egyptians. When you build a dam or a big house, people will come to help you. They will work free for you. The households will send food to feed the workmen. And when they build their houses, you will do the same for them.
>
> That's why the Pyramid was the national project of Egypt, because everyone had to participate in building this Pyramid ... [I]t was love—they were not really pushed to do it. When the king took the throne, the people had to be ready to participate in building the Pyramid. And when they finished it, they celebrated.[11]

Collapse of the Old Kingdom

The expensive and time-consuming building projects of the third and fourth dynasty could not last. The fifth dynasty witnessed the beginning of a small but important decline in the central power of the king and his vizier. Pyramids were still built, but they were much smaller than those at Giza, and successive pharaohs of the fifth and sixth dynasties increasingly turned to building temples to honor the sun god, Re. Also, toward the end of the fifth dynasty, there was a growing shift of power from the officials in the capital to the nobles who administered the provinces. Possibly due to "the result of a weakening centre," Charles Freeman wrote, "many administrative posts became hereditary and their holders [who before had dwelled in the capital] began to live on estates in the provinces they administered. This led to a gradual but inexorable decline in the authority of the kings. Now that they lived in the provinces, the nobles also built their own tombs there."[12]

A number of the wealthy men who built these provincial tombs ordered their biographies to be written on the walls. The reason was not entirely personal vanity. Such an account was also intended to show the gods that the man it described was worthy of entering the afterlife. For centuries, the accepted belief had been that only the king and a few close to him could gain eternal life; now, a new belief—that all people who led decent lives could make it to the afterlife—was emerging.

Because of these tomb biographies, the sixth dynasty is slightly better documented than the three that preceded

THE MEANING OF THE PYRAMID

V isitors to Egypt in both ancient and modern times have often asked why the early pharaohs and their builders chose the pyramidal shape for royal tombs. One reason was that the ancient mound of creation, the benben, which the Egyptians envisioned in their religious lore, was shaped roughly like a pyramid. Also, the ancient Egyptians viewed a pyramid in a symbolic sense as a special ramp or stairway. They believed that after a pharaoh died, his spirit would use that stairway to ascend into the heavens. A passage from the oldest known Egyptian funerary writings, the so-called Pyramid Texts, explained this: "A ramp to the sky is built for him [the pharaoh], that he may go up to the sky … He flies as a bird, and he settles as a beetle on an empty seat that is in the ship of Re [the sun god] … He has gone up into the sky and has found Re … He has taken his stand with Re in the northern part of the sky."[1]

1. Quoted in Josephine Mayer and Tom Prideaux, eds., *Never to Die: The Egyptians in Their Own Words*. New York, NY: Viking, 1938, pp. 43–44.

it. The writings reveal that during the Old Kingdom, the Egyptian government launched numerous military expeditions into Nubia, which was directly south of Egypt. These forays were designed to secure valuable goods, such as cattle and ivory, as well as to root out bandits who took refuge there. Brigands, generally referred to as rebels, also dwelled in the northern deserts west and east of the Nile Delta. Weni, a high official under three sixth dynasty pharaohs—Teti, Pepi I, and Merenra—recorded in his tomb how he led a large expedition against rebels in the northeastern deserts: "His Majesty sent me to lead this army five times, in order to repel … the Sand-Dwellers, each time they rebelled … I crossed over [in ships] … with these troops. I made a landing at the rear of the heights of the mountain range … I caught them all and every backslider [rebel] among them was slain."[13]

Partly because of the shift of power from the pharaoh's royal court in the capital to local rulers in the provinces, the government of the Old Kingdom became progressively weaker. Droughts and famines resulting from a series of unusually low Nile floods also contributed to the ongoing decline. Eventually, the central authority lost control of many of the provinces, and Egypt entered a period of serious political instability.

CHAPTER THREE

REUNIFICATION OF EGYPT

Following the near collapse of the government during the Old Kingdom was a period historians refer to as the First Intermediate Period, which was from the years 2130 to 1938 BC and spanned the dynasties 9, 10, and 11. During this time, Egypt had split off into regions. Memphis was still one of these important regions, but the kings resided in Heracleopolis, and that city was made the capital. Inscriptions from this time indicate that while the kings in Heracleopolis were acknowledged as being in control, their rule was actually not very powerful.

This time was filled with turmoil and rivalries between the different regions of Egypt, and this caused a great deal of instability on top of the poverty, famine, and drought that also occurred during this time. A document penned by a court scribe more than a century later, in more stable times, preserves a memory of the era of disunity:

I show you the land in turmoil. What should not be has come to pass. Men will seize weapons of warfare. The land will live in uproar … Each man's heart is for himself. Mourning is not done today. Hearts have quite abandoned it. A man sits with his back turned while one slays another. I show you the son as enemy, the brother as foe, a man slaying his father … The land [former country] has shrunk. Its rulers are many. It is bare. Its taxes are great.[14]

Although this time was marked by discontent and instability, one ruler was able to overcome rivals, remove the Heracleopolitans, and reunite Egypt. Mentuhotep II brought a time of stability, uniting Egypt under the Theban banner and bringing about the Middle Kingdom, which spanned the years 1938 to 1630 BC and the 12th and 13th dynasties.

Beginning of the Middle Kingdom

Mentuhotep II focused on unity and harmony during his reign, and he was successfully able to unite the regions of Egypt that had fallen to other rulers, such as the Heracleopolitans. With his rule and reunification of Egypt, he brought about the beginning of the Middle Kingdom. These themes of his rule can be seen in the special names he chose for himself and ordered to be inscribed on his monuments. "He who breathes life into the heart of the Two Lands" was the first name chosen and spoke of his desire to unify Egypt. The second name he chose for himself was "Divine is the White Crown." The white crown refers to the traditional headdress of the old king of southern Egypt; by invoking the ancient crown, this title stressed that Mentuhotep was from the South. The last was chosen 39 years into his reign, when he felt secure that Egypt had been united, and that was "He who unites the Two Lands." The Two Lands were Upper and Lower Egypt, now once again under the control of a single ruler. Having united all the nomes in the fertile Nile Valley, Mentuhotep eliminated or absorbed isolated pockets of nomads who had enjoyed an independent existence in the surrounding deserts for some time. Then, he extended his influence and power southward. He moved past Aswan, just north of the Nile's First Cataract. (The cataracts are places where the river suddenly changes elevation, causing turbulent rapids.) He next marched into northern Nubia, which once more became a valuable source of raw materials and luxury goods.

Mentuhotep II had a long and accomplished reign. He chose to celebrate it by creating for himself a large-scale funerary complex in the style of those of the leading Old Kingdom pharaohs. As in the distant and glorious past, ordinary Egyptians from far and wide gathered to build monuments to a single god-king. The great complex, located near Thebes, "began with a long causeway up from the edge of the desert," scholar Aidan Dodson wrote. It was "flanked at its upper end by trees and statues of the king. At its [lower] end lay a terraced building ... surmounted [topped] by a replica of the 'primeval mound' [a pyramid] from which all creation stemmed. Furnished with colonnades [rows of columns] and pillared halls, it was extensively decorated with scenes of religion and warfare."[15]

After Mentuhotep died and was laid to rest in his ornate burial complex, his son and then his grandson ruled Egypt. The latter, Mentuhotep IV, was succeeded by his own vizier, who was crowned as Amenemhat I, the first pharaoh of the 12th dynasty. The manner of the succession is unclear. Amenemhat may have engineered a palace coup and seized power by force, or Mentuhotep may have been childless and purposely chosen Amenemhat to succeed him.

However he came to power, Amenemhat, a strong and ambitious ruler, quickly tried to overshadow his immediate predecessors. A vigorous propaganda blitz made it appear as though the new king had fulfilled an earlier prophecy. Supposedly the prophecy had predicted the coming of a savior who would unite the warring factions of the chaotic First Intermediate Period, which took place between the Old Kingdom and Middle Kingdom timeframes:

This massive structure is the mortuary temple of Mentuhotep II; his powerful reign is reflected in the carefully built tomb.

Then a king will come from
  the South,
Ameny [Amenemhat], the justified …
He will take the white crown [of
  southern Egypt],
He will wear the red crown [of
  northern Egypt];
He will join the Two Mighty Ones
  [two gods representing the two
  halves of Egypt],
He will please the Two Lords with
  what they wish …
Rejoice, O people of his time,
The son of man will make his name
  for all eternity! …
Order will return to its seat,
While chaos is driven away.[16]

Amenemhat tried to take credit for the unification that Mentuhotep had already achieved. Regardless, Amenemhat was an effective and constructive ruler. In a gesture to tradition, Amenemhat kept Thebes as the country's administrative center. However, he built a new ceremonial capital at Itjtawy, located between Memphis and Meidum. Another important innovation of Amenemhat was the initiation of the tradition in which a pharaoh appointed his son co-regent (a sort of co-ruler) to help ensure a smooth transition of power when the father died. Thus, in 1965 BC, the crown prince, Senusret, became co-regent.

Establishing this plan for succession proved wise, as Amenemhat was assassinated in the 30th year of his reign. Senusret assumed full power

as Senusret I, and one of his first official acts was to order a court scribe to write an "instruction." A literary form that became popular in the Middle Kingdom, an instruction consisted of wise advice given by a father to his son. The document was worded as if it had been written by the dead king himself. It described his violent death and warned the new pharaoh to be on his guard and ready for any possible situation: "Beware of subjects who are nobodies, of whose plotting one is not aware … Trust not a brother, know not a friend; Make no intimates, [for] it is [a] worthless [effort]. When you lie down, guard your heart [and your body] yourself."[17]

Trade, Justice, and Learning in Egypt

Senusret and his successors of the 12th dynasty were well-meaning rulers who oversaw numerous building projects and made Egypt strong, safe, and prosperous. One of Senusret's own achievements was to build the earliest sections of what would later become the largest temple complex in the country. Located at Karnak, near Thebes, the site was sacred to Amun, an important god in Egyptian belief. One of Senusret's successors, Senusret II, oversaw a major expansion of croplands in the agricultural region surrounding Lake Faiyum. There, he built a small but impressive pyramid of brick. (Stone construction of pyramids was now abandoned, most likely because it was too expensive and time-consuming.) His son, Senusret III, also built a brick pyramid for his tomb. However, it was located in the more traditional burial area at Dahshur. The tomb of Senusret III was also different because it was his choice to return to the step-pyramid style made famous by Djoser in the early Old Kingdom.

The pharaohs of the 12th dynasty also expanded the country's volume of trade. A handful of foreign towns had been supplying Egypt with goods since the early years of the Old Kingdom. Especially crucial was Byblos, on the coast of what is now Lebanon, from which the Egyptians derived timber (particularly cedar), gold, and other valuable products. During the Middle Kingdom, trade with Byblos became so extensive that the locals adopted many Egyptian customs, including hieroglyphic writing.

The Egyptians also traded with the Minoans, who were an early, culturally advanced people occupying the Greek island of Crete. However, it appears that no formal trade links between Egypt and Mesopotamia existed at this time. This suggests that Egypt was still largely isolated from the outside world.

"FRAGILITY OF LIFE"

The Middle Kingdom had some stability and was reunified thanks to Mentuhotep II. However, there were other changes during this time as well. The architecture and art of this time period changed from massive pyramids to burial apartments and the art and literature depicted kings as more human:

> These kings were buried under pyramids, but they were not the massive, well-built structures of the past. Constructed instead of mud brick and cased only with stone, their burial apartments were complex mazes of corridors, designed perhaps in part to thwart robbers but also as models of the Underworld. It was in the Middle Kingdom that Amun, principal deity of the Theban region, first became important. The kings of this era erected temples at a cult center now known as Karnak on the east bank of the Nile at Thebes, where they worshipped Amun along with his consort, Mut, and their son, Khonsu. The art and literature of this period reflect a new awareness of the fragility of life, seen, for example, in the careworn and very human portraits of the later kings of the 12th dynasty.[1]

1. Zahi Hawass, *Tutankhamun and the Golden Age of the Pharaohs*. Washington, DC: National Geographic, 2011, p. 20.

Another hallmark of the Middle Kingdom was the adoption by many of its rulers of a moderate, enlightened style of rule that emphasized concepts such as forgiveness and justice. This is partly reflected in the famous surviving tale of Sinuhe, a minor official under the pharaoh Amenemhat I. After committing an infraction that made the king angry, Sinuhe fled Egypt and lived in Syria for a number of years. Homesick, the exile eventually returned and begged forgiveness of the pharaoh Senusret I, who generously restored Sinuhe to his former status. Another famous tale—that of the "Eloquent Peasant"—also demonstrated the fairness of the 12th dynasty pharaohs. After being cheated by a rich landowner, a poor peasant presented his case before a local magistrate. That official was so impressed by the peasant's eloquence, or speaking skill, that he brought the case before the king, who decided in favor of the poor man. "Justice is for eternity," the peasant said. "It enters the graveyard with its doer."[18] In time, this proved true, for most of the kings of the Middle Kingdom were later remembered as just rulers.

There was also a strong emphasis placed on learning in the Middle

EVOLUTION OF THE PYRAMID TEXTS

Some of the most valuable surviving artifacts that were found by archaeologists in the pyramids were the Pyramid Texts. These religious writings were meant for the kings to guide their journey to the afterlife and ensure their transformation into a god, and they evolved as Egyptian history evolved:

Chosen from a group of writings known collectively as netherworld texts, the scenes on the tomb walls and their associated labels developed out of the Pyramid Texts, older religious writings that had appeared first in Old Kingdom royal burial complexes. In the Middle Kingdom, these spells reappeared in a new form, as Coffin Texts inscribed on the inner walls of elite coffins. By the New Kingdom these mythological texts, with their associated illustrations, were painted on the walls of royal tombs and written on papyri. Not just collections of spells, as are found earlier, the New Kingdom texts are more coherent compositions that provide detailed images of the world beyond the Earth.[1]

1. Zahi Hawass, *Tutankhamun and the Golden Age of the Pharaohs*. Washington, DC: National Geographic, 2011, p. 117.

Senusret III was honored for his successful reign in this sculpture from the Middle Kingdom.

Kingdom, at least in upper-class circles. Most Egyptians remained poor and illiterate. However, scribes, or men who could read and write, created official documents for the government and taught others to do so. These scribes increased in number and importance. A well-known Middle Kingdom document known as the *Satire of Trades*, penned by one of these scribes for his students, described the great value of education:

> You must give yourself whole-
>   heartedly to learning,
>   [and thereby] discover what will
>   save you from the drudgery
>   of underlings.
>
> Nothing is so valuable as education;
>   it is a bridge over troubled waters …
>
> Let me urge you to love learning
>   more than your mother;
>   have its perfections enter
>   your mind.
>
> It is more distinguished than any
>   other occupation—
>   there is nothing like it upon Earth![19]

Development of the Military

Another notable development of the Middle Kingdom was an increase in the size and importance of Egypt's military. During the Middle Kingdom, the pharaohs maintained a larger army than had existed in the Old Kingdom.

This was probably in large part to discourage regional leaders from challenging the central government, a practice that had often led to civil strife and disunity in the past. At first, the troops were called up only when needed. Over time, increasing numbers of them served for extended time periods, either training or doing guard duty. Thus, although a full-time professional army was still not a reality, the basic elements of that institution were beginning to take shape.

The soldiers themselves were a mix of native-born Egyptians and men recruited from Nubia, which came increasingly under Egyptian control during the Middle Kingdom. To facilitate military expeditions to conquer and control that land, as well as to keep unwanted Nubians from entering Egypt, the government built numerous forts and fortified walls along the border. Senusret III was a particularly frequent fort builder. He also ordered the digging of an artificial channel that bypassed the First Cataract so that soldiers and traders could avoid the rapids.

With the increased emphasis on soldiering and forts, depictions of battles and other military themes became more common in the paintings and sculptures commissioned by the royal palace. Not surprisingly, the images of the pharaohs as strong military leaders were enhanced as well. Each successive ruler tried to present himself as an invincible hero, as in the case of

This mural shows Egyptians wielding weapons that would have been similar to the ones they used to wage war, including their powerful bows.

Senusret I. "He is a God, indeed, without peer," one of his fellow Egyptians wrote:

> He is a champion who acts with his own [arms], a fighter [like no one else] when he is seen attacking the [enemy] … [He] renders hands powerless, so that his enemies cannot muster their ranks. He is vengeful when he cracks skulls, and no one can stand up to him. He steps wide when he annihilates the fugitive … He is stalwart of heart … and he does not allow cowardice around him … The bowmen retreat before him as if before the might of a great goddess.[20]

The Hyksos Invade

Beginning in the 18th century BC, the Egyptian army ranks also started featuring young men of Near Eastern origins. This was the indirect result of political developments during the 13th and 14th dynasties. Most of the rulers of these dynasties had short reigns, contributing to a steady weakening of the central government. This caused control over the region east of the Nile Delta to grow lax, and over time, large numbers of immigrants from the eastern Mediterranean region settled there. Later Greek writers called these people the Hyksos, meaning "shepherd kings." For a while, the pharaohs

MILITARY STRATEGY AFTER THE HYKSOS INVASION

After the Hyksos invasion, the Egyptians realized they were no longer safe. They needed to expand their empire further to protect their land. To do this, they adopted a military strategy that consisted of two parts:

> First, each king marched south in order to secure his back and collect prisoners of war to serve in his armies. In this way Lower Nubia, and eventually Upper Nubia as well, became provinces of Egypt. After Nubia was "pacified," the pharaoh could turn his attention north and east and mount campaigns into Syria-Palestine. This empire building had the added benefits of guaranteeing trade routes and bringing in booty [goods] from foreign lands. New weaponry such as the duck-billed axe, the scimitar, and the chariot—all originally introduced by the Hyksos—helped to make the Egyptian armies formidable foes.[1]

1. Zahi Hawass, *Tutankhamun and the Golden Age of the Pharaohs*. Washington, DC: National Geographic, 2011, pp. 21–22.

tolerated these settlers and even used their young men as soldiers.

Eventually, the Hyksos grew more numerous and expanded westward and southward. By about 1650 BC, they had taken over Memphis and the rest of Lower Egypt. The Hyksos kings, who adopted Egyptian clothes, royal symbols, and customs, built their own capital, Avaris, in the eastern sector of the delta. There they established what later came to be designated the 15th and 16th dynasties.

Meanwhile, the Egyptian pharaohs, making up their own dynasty, the 17th, retreated to and maintained a power base in the South, centered on Thebes. These rulers became determined to rid the land of what they saw as foreign intruders. However, this could not be accomplished overnight, for the Hyksos were many in number and possessed a new military innovation they had acquired in Asia: the war chariot. In fact, it took almost a century for the Egyptians to rebound. Historians call this era in which the Hyksos occupied northern Egypt the Second Intermediate Period. It ended with the expulsion of the foreigners from Egypt, a major event in and of itself. However, its legacy was even more far-reaching, as Egyptian leaders now realized that the only way to keep the borders safe from future invaders was to go on the offensive. Egypt's great age of empire building was about to begin.

CHAPTER FOUR

THE CREATION OF AN EMPIRE

With the Hyksos being driven out of Egypt, the land was unified once again, and its rulers started the New Kingdom. The New Kingdom spanned the years 1539 to 1075 BC and encompassed the 18th, 19th, and 20th dynasties. This time also marked Egypt's great empires, which were a result of the Hyksos invasion. Egypt began to branch out and extend influence into other regions beyond its traditional borders, and therefore it also became a major military state during this time.

The ruler that brought in the new dynasty as well as a period of stability and unification was Ahmose, who ruled from 1539 to 1514 BC. Kamose ruled before him, but because Ahmose was a native ruler who reunified Egypt, he was considered the first pharaoh of the 18th dynasty.

The First Pharaohs of the New Kingdom

The New Kingdom began with strong leaders who reunified Egypt and led an equally strong military. The first pharaoh of the New Kingdom, Ahmose, brought about the 18th dynasty, which produced some of Egypt's most accomplished rulers. First, Ahmose led an army from Thebes and laid siege to the Hyksos capital, Avaris. This occurred about 10 years into Ahmose's reign. Following this siege and continuing a goal of creating an empire, he laid siege to Sharuhen in Palestine. The Middle East at this time did not have an established power, which allowed Ahmose to easily take it over and extend Egypt's influence. Ahmose's soldiers were rewarded with the spoils of war, including captives who later became slaves.

In addition to creating a strong military influence, Ahmose also established a government that was based on the Middle Kingdom, which made the vizier the highest judge in the realm and chief administrator, and created a new administration in the acquired territories. This new position was the overseer of southern foreign lands, which was second to the vizier. The person in this position was also given other powerful titles, making them deputy to the pharaoh himself.

Ahmose's actions set a precedent that most of his 18th dynasty successors followed. He was the first of a new set of pharaohs who were eager not only to make Egypt prosperous, but also to extend its influence and authority outward into foreign regions that earlier pharaohs had seen only as sources of trade. This aggressive method came to characterize and in some ways to define the image of Egyptian civilization during the early centuries of the New Kingdom. As one historian wrote,

> For the first time in history Egypt entered upon a path of continuing imperialism [empire building]. The Egyptian expansion abroad appears at times in contemporary records almost as a crusade to prove the power of Egyptian civilization. In modern psychological terms it has been called a compensation for the serious blow to native pride which had come in the Hyksos conquest.[21]

During the many military campaigns in this period, almost every pharaoh was eager to prove his capabilities as a warrior. As an invincible war hero and national savior, a pharaoh could be confident of keeping the allegiance of his people. Accordingly, the king's official image in royal decrees, building inscriptions, paintings, and other modes of propaganda was always a positive one. Every battle and campaign was portrayed as victorious, even when it had actually been a defeat or stalemate.

Sometimes the portrayal of a pharaoh's victory was described in words supposedly uttered by the god Amun-Re. A combination of the creator god Amun and the sun god Re, Amun-Re steadily emerged as the supreme deity of the New Kingdom. Typical of such propaganda was an inscription on a stele (stone marker or monument) set up at Karnak by the warlike pharaoh Thutmose III. Supposedly, Amun-Re proclaimed,

> My son, my champion, everlasting!
> I shine for love of you! ...
> I made your enemies succumb
>   beneath your soles,
> So that you crushed the rebels and
>   the traitors ...
> In might and victory ordained
>   by me ...
> I robbed their nostrils of the breath
>   of life ...
> My serpent on your brow consumed ...
>   the evildoers ...
> I let them see your majesty as lord
>   of light,
> so that you shone before them in
>   my likeness.[22]

The Reign of Hatshepsut

Although it was quite exaggerated, Thutmose III's Karnak inscription and other similar ones he commissioned did contain some truth. History proved him one of the strongest and most accomplished rulers of the 18th dynasty. He was also a product of the government policies and family politics of the pharaohs who immediately preceded him.

After Ahmose's successful military ventures into the eastern Mediterranean region, his successor, Amenhotep I, led military campaigns into Nubia and solidified Egypt's control of that region. The next pharaoh, Thutmose I, launched campaigns into both Nubia and Syria. Thutmose I also constructed a number of large buildings and monuments, including two obelisks at the growing Karnak temple complex.

One of Thutmose's sons by his wife Mutnefert succeeded him as Thutmose II. The latter took his half sister, Hatshepsut, as his chief wife. Thutmose II and Hatshepsut had a daughter together but no sons. However, the pharaoh did have a son with another wife. The boy was expected to succeed his father much later, when fully grown, but Thutmose died in 1479 BC when the crown prince was too young to rule. Hatshepsut assumed the position of regent for her stepson, the future Thutmose III, and became one of the few women ever to rule Egypt as pharaoh.

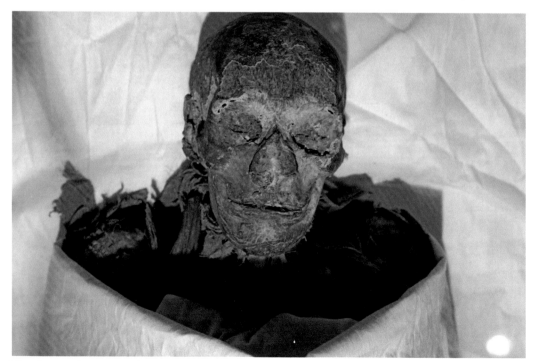

Hatshepsut's mummified remains are shown here.

Hatshepsut reigned until 1458 BC. During these years, the young Thutmose was technically her co-ruler, but it is likely that she allowed him little or no say in how the country was run. She was a vigorous leader who encouraged trade and sponsored numerous building projects. She is famous, for instance, for sending naval expeditions to Punt, a land south of Egypt on the African coast of the Red Sea. Her agents returned with plentiful supplies of incense, ebony wood, and cattle. Hatshepsut also rebuilt several temples and other structures that the Hyksos had damaged or destroyed, bragging in one of her inscriptions: "Hear ye, all persons! Ye people as many as ye are! … I have restored that which was ruins, I have raised up that which was unfinished since the Asiatics [the Hyksos] were in the midst of Avaris of the Northland, and the barbarians were in the midst of them, overthrowing that which was made, while they ruled in ignorance of Re."[23]

Hatshepsut also became renowned for her enormous mortuary temple at Dayr al-Baḥrī on the Nile's west bank across from Thebes. Consisting of two colonnaded terraces, it still survives in considerably good condition. In spite of her achievements, Hatshepsut was unable to maintain either power or a respected legacy in what was still a highly male-dominated society. Not only did Thutmose III succeed her on the throne

Located off the west bank of the Nile, this is the burial complex of Hatshepsut. It has survived the passage of time very well.

in 1458 BC, he also tried to erase all memory of her and her deeds. Her name was systematically and methodically removed from every monument she had erected. The exact reasons for this act are uncertain. Charles Freeman speculates that it "may be a sign of the spite of Thutmose for his powerful stepmother." However, more likely "the main objective was to restore an ordered and comprehensible past focused once again on male kingship."[24]

MYSTERY OF PUNT

There are plenty of mysteries surrounding ancient Egypt. However, one of them involves something that ordinarily would be quite hard to lose—an entire region. Historians and archaeologists are still quite unsure as to where the land of Punt actually was. Many theories have been suggested by historians, including Syria, Ethiopia, Arabia, Kenya, and others. Punt is one of the largest mysteries surrounding ancient Egypt because an entire land cannot simply go missing.

Punt was a region with which ancient Egyptians traded heavily for more than 1,000 years, and it produced gold, incense, and ebony. The Egyptians left plenty of evidence of the existence of the region. However, the location of the region itself is unknown, and no maps, directions, or distances to the land were ever left by the Egyptians. The most information given about the region was with Hatshepsut's expedition:

> Hatshepsut's expedition in the New Kingdom, if not the largest, was far and away the most thoroughly chronicled. Dispatched in the 15th century B.C., during the ninth year of her reign, the crusade is meticulously recorded on her bas-relief. One large scene portrays Punt itself, including beehive-shaped houses on stilts shaded by palm and possibly myrrh trees. Another scene depicts Hatshepsut's flotilla of ships departing for and arriving at the distant country, where they're "loaded very heavily with the marvels of the land of Punt" for the return voyage. A final scene shows dignitaries from Punt presenting their "marvels" to Queen Hatshepsut.[1]

In 2001, archaeological evidence was found that pointed to trade with the region at Saww, an ancient harbor site on the Red Sea. Here, ebony and obsidian products were found, in addition to cargo boxes with hieroglyphics that said the contents were the "wonders of Punt."

1. Peter Tyson, "Where Is Punt?," *NOVA*, December 1, 2009. www.pbs.org/wgbh/nova/ancient/egypt-punt.html.

Thutmose's Military Conquests

One traditional aspect of 18th dynasty kingship that Hatshepsut had neglected was the prosecution of large-scale military campaigns beyond Egypt's borders. Now that his stepmother was gone, Thutmose III corrected what he saw as a mistake with a vengeance. His conquests made Egypt's sphere of direct control and influence larger than it had ever been—about 400,000 square miles (1 million sq km), almost twice the size of the American state of Texas.

Thutmose's conquests were not simply a matter of his egotism and thirst for power. Rather, they were dictated by the political situation that existed in southwestern Asia during his reign. First, the young pharaoh sought to maintain dominance over the several independent city-states of the eastern Mediterranean region, as most of his immediate predecessors had. However, he also had to deal with a new and potentially dangerous enemy. Not long before he pushed Hatshepsut aside, he launched an attack on Megiddo.

Leading chariot and infantry units, Thutmose reached southern Syria, where he discovered that the enemy forces were using the city of Megiddo as a base. Against the advice of his leading officers, the pharaoh decided on a daring and risky surprise attack. At night, he led his troops through a narrow, dangerous mountain pass that descended onto the plain at a point only about 0.5 mile (0.8 km) from the city. Exiting the pass, the Egyptians surprised the Mitannian army, which was encamped outside the city's walls. Before the enemy troops could muster themselves and form proper ranks, Thutmose ordered a devastating charge. "Early in the morning, behold, command was given to the entire army to move," a passage from his royal records reads:

> His majesty went forth in a chariot of electrum [an alloy of gold and silver], arrayed in his weapons of war, like [the god] Horus, the Smiter, lord of power. . . . The southern wing of this army of his majesty was at the northwest of Megiddo while his majesty was in their center. . . . Then his majesty prevailed against them at the head of his army.[25]

Thutmose's victory was complete. Those enemy soldiers who were not slain by the onrushing Egyptians fled into Megiddo.

Victory at Mitanni

As part of his eighth military campaign, Thutmose marched into Mitanni with a large army. That army was considerably larger, more sophisticated, and more lethal than any that had existed during the Old and Middle Kingdoms. The armies fielded during the New Kingdom were made up of a mixture of units, each featuring a specific kind of fighter and weaponry. The centerpiece of the army was the chariot corps.

ROYAL TOMBS

An Egyptian tomb had two parts that consisted of the burial chamber, which was generally below ground, and the chapel, which was above. The placement of the chapel above ground served a purpose, and the decoration of the chapel was to reproduce the rituals and offerings for eternity. The ancient Egyptians believed that upon death, the ba and ka, which were the two main parts of a person's identity, separated. "The ka was the life force, perhaps the most crucial part of a person's identity. In order to function in the afterlife, the ka in its tomb … needed food, drink, incense, clothing, and perpetual ritual care. The ba can be understood as the soul or personality."[1]

The mummified body of the king was seen as a vessel where the ba could dwell eternally, and if something happened to the mummy, the statues in the tomb could be substitutes for the physical vessel of the mummy. Additionally,

> The purpose of the royal tomb was to protect the royal body and, in conjunction with the cult temple near the floodplain, to guarantee the eternal life of the king and the continuance of the universe. The soul of the deceased king would hear the rituals and receive offerings within the mortuary temple, then return to the body within the tomb, symbolically slipping below the horizon to brave the dangers of the night world and join with Osiris before being reborn at dawn.[2]

An Egyptian casket is shown here, located in the middle of a highly decorated and elaborately constructed royal tomb.

1. Zahi Hawass, *Tutankhamun and the Golden Age of the Pharaohs*. Washington, DC: National Geographic, 2011, p. 115.
2. Zahi Hawass, *Tutankhamun and the Golden Age of the Pharaohs*, pp. 115–116.

By Thutmose's day, the Egyptian war chariot had become a mobile platform from which a warrior fired arrows from a composite bow or hurled metal-tipped javelins. The composite bow had much more elasticity and power than traditional, simple bows. This was because the simple bow was made from a single piece of wood, whereas the composite bow was composed of several diverse materials, including two or three varieties of wood, animal horn, animal tendons, and glue. In a large-scale battle, the charioteers, armed with their composite bows and javelins, charged at the enemy ranks. They did not make actual contact, however. Egyptian chariots were extremely lightweight and could not withstand the shock of crashing into a line of foot soldiers, or infantry. Instead, the charioteers unleashed their arrows, creating a deadly rain, and then wheeled around for a second charge to take advantage of the confusion.

Meanwhile, the Egyptian chariots were supported by units of their own infantry, often called runners. Among them were foot-archers and soldiers wielding battle-axes, swords, and spears. The bulk of the infantry was now made up of native Egyptians. However, similarly to past ages, foreign-born fighters still supplemented the ranks. These included Nubians, Libyans, and others who had been captured and forced to fight for Egypt. As a rule, the foot soldiers followed the chariots into battle. As the fight progressed, the infantrymen cleared the field of destroyed chariots, captured or killed fallen enemy charioteers, rescued their own fallen charioteers, and chased after fleeing enemy troops.

Prosperity Under Amenhotep III

After his great victory, Thutmose sought a way to maintain control over the eastern Mediterranean region without keeping tens of thousands of troops stationed there, which would have been far too expensive. He took the sons of local rulers back to Egypt as hostages. For fear of losing their sons, these rulers remained loyal to Egypt rather than Mitanni. In addition, the hostages were taught Egyptian ideas and customs and later sent back to their home cities to become controlled rulers who were friendly to Egypt.

The hostility between Egypt and Mitanni eventually dissipated, however. One of Thutmose's successors, his grandson Thutmose IV, made an alliance with Mitanni. This alliance was further cemented when the son and successor of Thutmose IV, Amenhotep III, took the daughter of a Mitannian ruler as his bride.

In the view of most historians, the New Kingdom reached its height of prosperity and splendor during Amenhotep III's long reign. This was partly because the country operated smoothly under an efficient bureaucracy. The government was divided into departments, each run by a group of officials who reported directly to the pharaoh. Under these officials were the governors of provinces and mayors of towns. Amenhotep also greatly expanded the massive temple complex at Karnak and built most of the Luxor Temple, which was located nearby.

The two sacred sanctuaries were joined by a long avenue lined with stone sphinxes.

These temples were dedicated to Amun-Re and other traditional gods, whose cults were supreme in Egyptian

worship. During Amenhotep's reign, however, a more obscure cult began to gain increasing numbers of followers. The pharaoh showed a good deal of interest in the god of this cult—Aten—but not at the expense of the traditional gods, which he continued to support. He had no way of knowing that his successor would create a religious revolution based on the worship of Aten and, in doing so, would shake the foundations of Egyptian civilization.

The Luxor Temple, one of the most ambitious building projects of the ancient world, has inspired countless artists and historians.

CHAPTER FIVE

THE NEW KINGDOM

Much of what is known of the New Kingdom is centered on royalty and the wealthy, and this is based on paintings and other artifacts that have been found in tombs. While these objects and artwork mainly focus on religion and have mortuary significance, these artifacts also provide a lot of information on the daily lives of ancient Egyptians.

Floor plans of palaces have been found, and for more than 100 years, archaeologists have been excavating Deir el-Medina. They have found evidence of what food was eaten, court trials, literature, and more. Additionally, what has been found shows that the ancient Egyptians were not so different from people today. They were engineers, they raised families, they were sometimes traitors and thieves, and they were sometimes content with their position in life and sometimes jealous of their neighbors. Also, in ancient Egypt, women had a higher status and could represent themselves in a court of law and own property.

While the royal and elite lived a life of luxury, the middle class also aspired to live a life of privilege. The elite had fine linen clothing, wore jewels made of semiprecious stones and gold, and wore wigs and cosmetics on their cheeks, lips, and eyes. Even though they did not have the means that the upper class did, the middle class also wore jewels, wigs, and fine clothing and commissioned coffins and other funerary goods. Overall, what these excavations indicate is the importance of the home in the structure of Egyptian life.

Food and Housing

Historians agree that the family and home supported Egyptian society. Although many families consisted of a father, mother, and their children, some also included grandparents, uncles, aunts, cousins, and in-laws sharing the same living space. Thus,

The Deir el-Medina ruins have been an excellent source for knowledge of the New Kingdom of Egypt.

family size could vary considerably. Likewise, the size, layout, and facilities of the houses these families lived in varied widely.

While many Egyptians lived in villages, during the time period of the New Kingdom, larger towns and cities began to rise in popularity. Each house was made of mud brick, and occasionally, doorjambs would be made of stone. Whether a citizen was wealthy or lived in poverty, however, one thing was common: They chose to live on high ground to stay out of the area of the yearly flood of the Nile River.

Those who lived in poverty generally lived in a hut with one room. Families lived in houses with many rooms that served the same functions as houses do today—there were rooms for sleeping, eating, cooking, storage, and seeing visitors. The elite lived in complex houses, often villas or small estates, with bakeries and manufacturing areas in addition to the standard rooms of a house. While the houses were not furnished with many material goods, most houses often had a shrine to a god or ancestor.

Just as the housing and family situations in the New Kingdom were different, the food the Egyptians ate was also varied:

[The diet's] staples were bread and beer, made from wheat and barley. Vegetable gardens yielded lettuce, onions, leeks, garlic, and ... lentils or peas. Many different fruits were available, including ... Egyptian plums, fruit from the dom palm, sycamore figs, and dates and grapes, which were both eaten and used for wine. Fish were an important food source for all levels of society; in addition to being eaten fresh, their flesh and eggs were dried and salted for longer-term storage.

Domesticated and captured wild animals were kept in pens, where they were fed, cared for, bred, and then eaten. Cattle were highly valued as an important source of meat, eaten mostly by the elite and those laboring for the king. The Egyptians consumed sheep, goats, and pigs (although the last were considered low-status animals), and drank milk plain or made it into yogurt or cheese. They also enjoyed eggs and meats from all sorts of poultry.[26]

The Rights of Women and Slaves

Ancient Egypt was ahead of its time when it came to women's rights and gender equality. Although men were socially superior, women had the same legal rights as men did. An ancient Egyptian woman could own, inherit, and give away land and other property, as well as enter into legally binding contracts. A woman could also sue someone in court. In addition, women enjoyed complete freedom of movement, which allowed large numbers of them to work outside the home. Egyptian women were

THE IMPORTANCE OF GOLD

Egyptians had a wealth of raw materials available for their use, which allowed them to create much of their funerary objects and allowed craftsmen to perfect their practice with materials such as wood, stone, ceramic, metal, glass, and most importantly, gold. The Egyptians referred to gold as "the flesh of the gods," and this material was found north of Thebes along the Eastern Desert to the Fourth Cataract in Nubia. It was easily extracted from the earth through shallow surface mines and could be melted into ingots and traded for other luxury materials.

Gold was not only in abundance in the region, it was also easy to work with:

It can be manipulated cold, and does not tarnish. It was a perfect metal for intricate jewels and other objects meant to last for eternity. Ideally, mummies were clothed in gold in the form of golden or gilded coffins, creating a divine, immutable skin for the deceased. A number of different techniques were used to create masterpieces such as those found with Tutankhamun. Protected by layers of leather or papyrus, sheets of varying thicknesses were hammered out using stone beaters against a stone anvil. Thicker sheets, cut into pieces that were then shaped and soldered together, could be used for objects such as vessels and jewelry. Thinner sheets … [decorated] the exteriors of coffins, statues, and the like … Gold was sometimes (although less commonly) heated and poured into molds: Some objects were cast using the lost-wax method, in which a model of the object was made of wax, coated with clay, then heated so that the wax melted and flowed out, leaving behind an empty mold.[1]

Gold was considered to be closely related to the gods. Therefore, it was seen as a perfect material for pharaohs, such as Tutankhamun (depicted in the burial mask shown here), to be buried with.

1. Zahi Hawass, *Tutankhamun and the Golden Age of the Pharaohs*. Washington, DC: National Geographic, 2011, pp. 57–60.

also allowed to seek divorce, and the woman kept all property she brought to the marriage. Before marriage, a man and woman in ancient Egypt could create a prenuptial agreement, which is a contract stating what property each person brought into the marriage and what would happen to it in case the man and woman divorced. In case a divorce did happen, the wife would be taken care of if she signed a prenuptial agreement.

One artifact that has been found is a 2,480-year-old prenuptial agreement that is 8 feet (2.4 m) long. The document ensured the woman would be provided for if a divorce happened, and part of this included 36 bags of grain a year for the rest of her life.

Whatever the reasons for divorce, such family breakups were rare in ancient Egypt. One of the reasons may have been that both fathers and mothers strongly desired and felt obliged to stay with and raise their children. This was because all Egyptians, whether rich or poor, took great pride in their families. Evidence found in the ruins of the workers' village at Deir el-Medina indicates that most of the families there had one, two, or three children. This suggests a ratio of children per household similar to that in modern developed countries such as the United States, although it is possible that the sizes of the families at Deir el-Medina were not typical for Egypt as a whole.

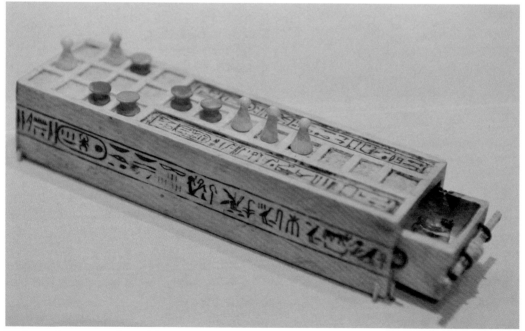

This antique game board is constructed from ivory; it represents what some toys looked like in ancient Egypt.

When they were old enough, the children of Deir el-Medina and other Egyptian towns played with toys, including dolls, puppets, spinning tops, and miniature weapons. The latter included replica swords, axes, bows and arrows, and chariots. Balls were also widely popular, and depictions of a wide variety of ball games have survived in paintings and sculptures. Children's lives did not consist only of play, however. Around the age of 14, boys would start helping their fathers in their profession. Similarly, young women helped their mothers cook, clean, and make clothes. In general, children were expected to obey their parents and other adults. It was also expected that a good son or daughter would help care for their parents in their old age.

Some Egyptian families also had live-in slaves. The number of slaves kept by the ancient Egyptians is unclear; in fact, historians are frequently unable to tell the difference between free servants and truly enslaved individuals in the surviving records. This is because ancient Egyptian slaves did not lack all civil and legal rights. Although Egyptian slaves toiled hard at menial jobs and could be bought, sold, or rented out, they possessed certain basic rights. The treatment of slaves seems to have varied widely; many masters treated their household slaves like members of the family, while some slave owners abused their slaves.

Jobs in Ancient Egypt

Although slaves did a certain amount of the difficult physical labor in ancient Egypt, evidence indicates that most of the jobs in the country were held by free people. By far the most common occupation, as it was throughout the ancient world, was farming. During the planting season, farmers scattered their seeds by hand and then used wooden plows drawn by cattle or donkeys to work the seeds into the soil. Because the soil laid down by the yearly Nile floods was so rich and pliable, some farmers did not need to plow. They had pigs, goats, and other farm animals trample the seeds into the soil. During the spring harvest, field workers cut down the crops, and then assistants picked up the fallen crops and loaded them into baskets.

Another common occupation during Egypt's New Kingdom was soldiering, mainly because thousands of troops were on active duty at any given time during this period. Most soldiers entered the profession by following in their fathers' footsteps. After a man joined the army, his name was added to lists that were kept from one generation to the next, and when he retired or died in the line of duty, his son took his place. Often new recruits were lured into joining the army by the prospect of collecting treasures. As a rule, a victorious pharaoh shared the gold, jewels, horses, slaves, and other valuables he acquired during a campaign with his troops. Also, soldiers were allowed

Ancient Egypt has been a fascination for many throughout the years, especially since the discovery of King Tutankhamun's tomb in 1922 by Howard Carter. This fascination has crossed over into popular culture, especially in books and movies. Egyptian gods are featured in Rick Riordan's 2010 fiction series the Kane Chronicles, which follows the main characters Sadie and Carter, who are descended from the pharaoh Narmer. Ancient Egypt was also the theme of the 1994 science fiction movie, *Stargate*, in which a teleportation device is found in Egypt and the main characters are transported to a place where people worship the god Re. Mummies have also been featured extensively in movies, from 1932's *The Mummy* with Boris Karloff, to 1999's *The Mummy* with Brendan Fraser, which kicked off several sequels, and 2017's remake of *The Mummy* with Tom Cruise.

However, while these fictional accounts are entertaining, nothing compares to the actual history of ancient Egypt, and *National Geographic* has allowed thousands of people across the world to experience the wonder of this time through their traveling exhibitions. These traveling exhibitions have featured Tutankhamun and Cleopatra and toured with actual artifacts found in the pyramids' tombs, such as statues, jewelry, ritual jars, mummies, and even a sarcophagus.

This gold statue of Tutankhamun is just one part of countless exhibits that showcase ancient Egypt.

to keep any prisoners they personally captured as slaves. However, a soldier's life was often difficult. In wartime, there were long marches through barren regions; periods of hunger, thirst, and little sleep; backbreaking work setting up and taking down camp; and harsh discipline. A surviving Egyptian document designed to encourage men to become scribes rather than soldiers described many of the common hazards of military campaigning in the ancient world:

He drinks water every third day. It is smelly and tastes of salt. His body is ravaged by illness. The enemy comes, surrounds him with [arrows], and life recedes from him … His wife and children are in their village; he dies and does not reach it. If he comes out alive, he is worn out from marching … If he leaps [runs away] and joins the deserters, all his people [family members] are imprisoned … Be a scribe and be spared from soldiering![27]

Although a large proportion of Egyptian men were either farmers or soldiers, many other jobs were filled by male workers. Among others, these included fishermen, miners, quarrymen, carpenters, potters, stone masons, and merchants. Many of these professions required considerable skills and training. However, the vast majority of these workers were seen as socially inferior by members of the upper classes. Typical of this attitude is this passage from a surviving document that characterizes the potter's profession as dirty and degrading to the craftsman:

*The potter with his earth and clay—
    he rises early with the servants;
Weeds and swine hinder his efforts
    until he manages to fire his pots.
His clothing is stiff with slime [from the wet clay]
    and his leather apron is in tatters.
The air which enters up his nose
    spews directly from his kiln.[28]*

Men were not the only workers in ancient Egypt, however, as many women also held jobs. Some labored in workshops where fabric was spun and clothes made, and others were assistants to bakers or millers. Other common female professions included hairdressing and entertaining, including singing, dancing, and playing musical instruments. The royal court, the mansions of wealthy landowners, and large temple complexes all hired troupes of female entertainers.

Worship of the Gods

Regardless of their wealth, the size of their home, their social status, or their occupation, nearly all ancient Egyptians were deeply religious. The Egyptians believed that a number of powerful deities existed and held sway over nature and humanity. It was thought that one or more gods controlled or influenced nearly every aspect of the natural world and daily life. For example, Egyptians believed Hapy made the Nile flood each year and inspired the growth of crops and other plants. Isis was one of the most important goddesses and was a role model for women, cured the sick, and was connected with rites of the dead. The goddess Hathor, generally depicted with a cow's head or cow's ears, was associated with celebration, joy, and matters dealing with love.

The Egyptians believed that these and other gods had to be worshiped and appeased on a regular basis, or else humanity might suffer from divine wrath. Most public worship took place at traditional religious festivals held at set times of the year. Some of these ceremonies were attended by thousands of people who journeyed from far and wide to watch priests from local temples conduct large-scale sacrifices and recite prayers. The sacrifices consisted of material gifts offered to a god or gods.

Another crucial aspect of ancient Egyptian religion was the belief that,

NEGATIVE CONFESSIONS

The Egyptians had many rituals designed to ensure they would make it to the afterlife. One of these involved confessing their sins or denying that they had committed any sins. Supposedly these actions appeased the gods. One common confession was the negative confessional. It consisted of a series of statements, each swearing that a specific sin had not been committed. Many Egyptians memorized it so that after they died they would be prepared to recite it to Osiris and the other divine judges. Part of the negative confession reads:

I have not done crimes against people. I have not mistreated cattle. I have not sinned in the Place of Truth [a temple or cemetery] … I have not blasphemed a god. I have not robbed the poor. I have not done what the god abhors … I have not caused tears. I have not killed … I have not damaged the offerings in the temples … I have not taken milk from the mouths of children … I have not held back water in its season. I have not dammed a flowing stream.[1]

1.   Quoted in Miriam Lichtheim, ed., *Ancient Egyptian Literature: A Book of Readings, vol. 2.* Berkeley, CA: University of California Press, 2006, pp. 124–126.

This painting shows the young Tutankhamun participating in one of the many Egyptian religious rituals.

following death, people who had led decent lives would live for eternity in the afterlife. To make it to the next life required following a number of strict, ancient burial rituals. This is why the Egyptians devoted so much time and energy to burial customs, such as reciting prayers and spells; confessing sins; preserving the body through embalming, or mummification; preparing proper tombs or gravesites; conducting solemn and sometimes elaborate funerals; and bringing offerings of food and other gifts to gravesites long after the funerals. Thus, a great deal of time in the life of an average Egyptian was spent thinking about or preparing for death.

CHAPTER SIX

RELIGIOUS REFORM

While Amenhotep III was remembered as a great builder, his successor, Amenhotep IV, was remembered for the amount of deconstruction he did on one of Egypt's most important institutions: religion. Amenhotep IV started a religious revolution that was centered on the sun god, Aten, instead of Amun-Re. Amenhotep IV even went so far as to change his name to Akhenaten, which means "One useful to Aten." He did such damage that many successors tried to erase his memory from Egyptian records.

However, their efforts failed. Akhenaten's religious ideas, physical monuments, and images in art were too many to be eradicated completely. Moreover, the widespread hatred he inspired in most of his subjects ensured that he would be remembered. His reign, now often called the Amarna age or period, after the name of the new capital he created, became a stain that Egyptian civilization could not remove. According to one scholar, "[he] had brought the country and its people to the very brink of disaster,"[29] and inspired a hatred that kept the king's memory alive in the cultural consciousness for generations to come.

Establishment of Aten

Akhenaten created trouble and inspired rage among his people by eliminating the worship of the traditional gods and replacing them with the cult and worship of a single deity. This god was Aten, most often represented as the sun's bright disk. The basic concept of Aten was actually nothing new. Well before the advent of the New Kingdom, the Egyptians used the term Aten to describe the sun's physical manifestation. However, this was considered to be separate from the sun god himself—Re, later worshiped as Amun-Re. During the early years of the New Kingdom, this view of Aten began to change. During the reigns of Thutmose IV and Akhenaten's father, Amenhotep III, both priests and ordinary people came to think of Aten as a deity separate from, though closely connected to, Amun-Re.

Akhenaten did not invent the idea of Aten's divinity. If he had merely worshiped that god along with Amun-Re and other traditional gods, as his predecessors had, no one would have objected. Akhenaten's controversial approach was to claim that Aten was the only true god. Not long after his father's death, the young pharaoh ordered worship of the old gods to be abandoned in favor of the cult of Aten. He even went so far as to send out men armed with chisels and mallets to carve away all written mentions of the former chief god, Amun-Re. It was during this early part of his reign that Amenhotep IV also honored the one god by changing his name to Akhenaten.

The reasons behind this extreme and controversial policy are still uncertain. Some historians have suggested that Akhenaten was a sincere religious reformer, the world's first major monotheist (someone who believes that there is just one god). A few have even speculated that the Biblical figure Moses, who was supposedly raised as an Egyptian prince, based the idea of the sole Hebrew god on Akhenaten's vision of Aten. Many scholars are skeptical, however. As Freeman pointed out, the pharaoh might have had political as well as religious motives: "He may simply have been trying to assert his own independence from the power of the temples."[30] Whatever motivated Akhenaten, he did close down most or all the temples of the traditional gods, confiscated gold and other valuables, and seized large and lucrative estates. It is hardly surprising, therefore, that the influential priests of these temples became enemies of a ruler they viewed as dangerous.

Worshiping Aten

The new cult the traditional priests hated so much was built on the idea that Aten, the sole god, had created the universe and now watched over Egypt. Moreover, depictions of Aten in paintings and relief sculptures suggest that this deity had a personal connection with the reigning pharaoh and his family.

Akhenaten and those who followed him in his new faith employed the same basic rituals that Egyptians had used in worship for countless generations: prayer and sacrifice. Some ancient Egyptian prayers were repeated so often that they became standard hymns that worshipers recited or sang from memory. A hymn to Aten has survived, with versions discovered in the tombs of five of Akhenaten's court members. Possibly written by the pharaoh himself, the hymn praises Aten as the creator of the world, humanity, animals, and plants and as a being who inspires love and joy in his worshipers.

Akhenaten is shown here worshipping Aten in this slab that was made during the New Kingdom.

One of the passages from the hymn is as follows:

> Splendid you rise, O living Aten,
>   eternal lord!
> You are radiant, beauteous, mighty.
> Your love is great, immense.
> Your rays light up all faces,
> Your bright hue gives light to hearts,
> When you fill the Two Lands [Egypt]
>   with your love.
> August God who fashioned himself,
> Who made every land, created what
>   is in it,
> All peoples, herds, and flocks,
> All trees that grow from soil …
> Every heart acclaims your sight,
> When you are risen as their lord.[31]

Akhenaten also honored Aten by building temples for him. The first was at Thebes, not far from the Karnak religious complex. The pharaoh came to view this as too close to the symbols of the old faith, however, and he built another temple to Aten north of Thebes. This new temple, called the House of Aten, no longer exists because Akhenaten's enemies destroyed it after his death. However, the tombs of some of the pharaoh's chief followers have preserved information about Aten's cult. Paintings on the walls of these tombs show detailed depictions of the temple complex, which featured two major and distinct structures. The first, which the faithful called "the place where the Aten is found," had a large open courtyard containing many table-like altars.

It is believed that the pharaoh and his priests placed sacrificial offerings to Aten on these altars. The second structure was a raised platform bearing a sacred stone. Thus, unlike the situation in traditional temples, where the sacred statues rested in enclosed, darkened chambers, the temple featured outdoor worship directed upward toward the sun's disk.

The Amarna Temple

This open-air temple was one of the centerpieces of the new capital Akhenaten built in the early years of his reign. He called it Akhetaten, meaning "Horizon of Aten." Today it is known as Amarna, after the Arabic name for the area in which it was unearthed: Tell el Amarna. In addition to temples, Amarna had government buildings, shops, townhouses for the king's administrators and courtiers, residential housing for the artisans and other workers, and adjoining stretches of farmland to provide a ready supply of food. Tombs for Amarna's nobles—in which the copies of Aten's hymn were found—were carved out of a series of rocky cliffs that partially surrounded the city.

There was also a palace for the pharaoh and his family. The king's chief wife, Nefertiti, bore him six daughters, and the seven women were frequently depicted in palace art. According to discovered artifacts, Nefertiti was a beautiful woman whom Akhenaten deeply loved. This is revealed in surviving paintings of the two embracing and

Akhenaten and Nefertiti were depicted in much of the artwork around the palace. Shown here are two surviving busts of Akhenaten (left) and Nefertiti (right).

even kissing, a level of intimacy almost never depicted in Egyptian art in other periods. The pharaoh also had at least two sons. One, Tutankhaten, later succeeded his father on the throne. He was probably born of a lesser wife, Kiya.

Also prominent in the art of the Amarna court are seemingly realistic portrayals of Akhenaten that are different from the standard, stylized depictions of Egyptian pharaohs. As a rule, these rulers were portrayed as young, physically healthy, and perfectly proportioned, even when they were old or infirm in reality. In most of the paintings and sculptures of Akhenaten, however, his body looks deformed in various ways. According to Lionel Casson, these images of the pharaoh "give him an elongated jaw, scrawny neck, drooping shoulders, potbelly, [and] spindly legs."[32] A number of explanations have been offered to explain these odd depictions of Akhenaten. Some scholars suggest that he suffered from some sort of debilitating physical condition, perhaps a rare genetic disorder. As of 2017, the most widely accepted theory is that he suffered from Marfan syndrome, the symptoms of which include a long face, elongated limbs and fingers, curvature of the spine, and a wide pelvis.

Whatever his personal infirmities or problems, Akhenaten managed, with the aid of his vizier and other assistants, to continue to expand his new capital. The pharaoh also maintained a lively correspondence with the rulers of other Near Eastern lands, including Mitanni, Assyria, Babylonia, and Hatti (what is now Turkey). Some of these letters, carved onto clay tablets in Akkadian, which was then the international language of diplomacy, have survived. Because they were found in the ruins of Amarna, historians call them the Amarna Letters. A typical example is one of several letters written to Akhenaten by Burnaburiash, king of Babylonia. The latter complained that some of his agents and merchants had been robbed and killed in the eastern Mediterranean region, then controlled by Egypt:

> To [Akhenaten] … king of Egypt … Thus speaks Burnaburiash King of Babylon, your brother. I am well. To your country, your house, your women, your sons, your ministers, your horses, your chariots, many greetings … And now, my merchants who travelled … [in the Near East] for business … [Men working for a local ruler] beat my merchants and stole their money … [This region] is your country and its kings are your slaves … [I ask you to] bind them and return the money they robbed. And the men who murdered my slaves, kill them and avenge their blood. Because if you do not kill these men, they will again murder my caravans and even my ambassadors, and the ambassadors between us will cease.[33]

The End of Amarna

The letter from the Babylonian king hints that during Akhenaten's reign,

A tablet containing one of the Amarna Letters is shown here; they consisted of correspondence between Akhenaten and rulers of other lands.

Egypt had become somewhat weak in policing its empire in the eastern Mediterranean region. The same sort of governmental neglect may have prevailed in many parts of Egypt outside of Amarna—not that most Egyptians cared about the pharaoh and his attentions anyway. At the very least, many priests, nobles, and ordinary people in various parts of Egypt were disgusted by his abandonment of the traditional gods. "The impact was profound," one scholar wrote:

> Many temples were closed down ... and the masses lost their [religious] festivals. As the reign went on, the persecution of [Amun-Re] became more intense ... [But] for the mass of people there was no incentive to turn away from traditional religious practices which were so deeply integrated into everyday life ... To replace [the traditional gods] by a single physical entity ... was a cultural shock far greater than the Egyptians could absorb. Even the workmen building [Amarna] stayed loyal to their traditional gods.[34]

The result was that when Akhenaten died in the 17th year of his reign, his detractors far outnumbered his supporters. It was therefore inevitable that his unpopular religious revolution could not survive. As one scholar described it: "With the disappearance of Akhenaten's charismatic presence ... the whole Amarna edifice came tumbling down

for good."[35] Now the reinstated priests of Amun-Re could try to erase Aten's name from the monuments. Meanwhile, the once-bustling city of Amarna was abandoned.

The Boy-King

This rollback of Akhenaten's religious ideas and abandonment of his new capital did not happen all at once. After the pharaoh's death, there was a brief transition period in which his immediate successors accepted a return to worshiping Amun-Re and the old gods but were reluctant to cease worshiping Aten altogether. The idea of having Aten and Amun-Re coexist as leading divinities may have been the idea of the country's most powerful royal adviser, Ay. However, regardless of who thought of this policy, it ultimately destroyed all the powerful government figures who promoted it.

Today, the most famous of these figures is Akhenaten's son and second successor, Tutankhaten, who was given the nickname King Tut after his gold-filled tomb was discovered in 1922 by archaeologist Howard Carter. The real first successor of the unpopular pharaoh, however, was an obscure person named Smenkhare. He may have been a little-known brother or son of Akhenaten, and he ruled only a few months and then disappeared, leaving the throne to Tutankhaten, who was then about eight years old.

The boy-king's birth name meant "living image of Aten." However, Ay

Tutankhaten, also known as Tutankhamun (shown here in this piece of a statue), is undoubtedly ancient Egypt's most famous ruler, despite his short time on the throne.

A FAMOUS DISCOVERY

In 1922, English archaeologist Howard Carter made one of the most sensational finds of the 20th century—the long-forgotten tomb of the Egyptian boy-king Tutankhamun. What made the find so famous was not Tut himself, for he was an obscure ruler who accomplished little and died young. Rather, the treasure trove of grave goods in the tomb was still largely intact, whereas the valuables in most other pharaohs' tombs had been looted by thieves. Tutankhamun's tomb contained, among many other priceless artifacts, hunting and sports equipment, including bows, arrows, bronze swords, gold daggers, shields, and full-sized chariots; several musical instruments; and furniture, including chairs, stools, beds, storage chests, and a gold throne. Most incredible of all was a series of three coffins. Each was nested within another and the innermost one, containing Tutankhamun's mummy, was made of pure gold. On the boy-king's face, Carter found a magnificent gold mask studded with precious stones. Tutankhamun's arms were crossed, and his hands held the crook and flail, traditional symbols of the ancient Egyptian kings.

In all, 5,000 items were discovered in King Tutankhamun's tomb. Some of these artifacts have traveled around the world, but not all pieces have been displayed together. However, that changed in 2018 with the opening of the Grand Egyptian Museum, which is located near the Pyramids of Giza. For the first time, each of the 5,000 pieces are displayed together in 4 rooms, much as they were in King Tutankhamun's tomb. Additionally, many objects have been publicly displayed for the first time, such as clothing pieces that were determined to be too fragile to travel.

Since the discovery of Tutankhamun's tomb and the treasures within, Egyptian studies have become even more popular.

was in charge of the government due to Tut's age and advised the new pharaoh to change his name. Ay and the other royal advisers thought this would help appease the many supporters of Amun-Re. Thus, Tutankhaten became Tutankhamun, meaning "living image of Amun." However, Tutankhamun also maintained his ties to his father's court and regime by marrying one of Akhenaten's daughters, Ankhesenamun.

Tutankhamun reigned nine years. He may have been murdered in a palace plot, although most scholars now think he died from a head injury sustained in an accidental fall. However the boy-king died, Ay made sure that he received a proper funeral. Then,

Howard Carter's discovery of King Tut's tomb is one of the greatest historical finds of all time.

Ay made himself pharaoh and married Tutankhamun's young widow, Ankhesenamun. However, like his young predecessor, Ay was too tainted by his connections to the hated Akhenaten to enjoy any popularity as a ruler. Four years after he took the throne, he was dead—and a powerful military general, Horemheb, had taken his place.

A traditionalist and supporter of Amun-Re, Horemheb ordered the names of Akhenaten, Nefertiti, Smenkhare, Tutankhamun, and Ay to be chiseled off all monuments. He even forbade people from speaking their names. The new pharaoh hoped that normal life would be restored and that history would quickly forget those who had dared to challenge Egypt's old gods. The irony is that over the course of more than 3,000 years, the opposite happened. Today, Tutankhamun is the best known of all the pharaohs, and many people consider Akhenaten to be one of the most fascinating.

CHAPTER SEVEN

EGYPT'S NEW ENEMIES

The 18th dynasty ended with Horemheb. The first rulers of the 18th dynasty expanded Egypt's empire until Akhenaten ruled and was greatly disliked by many Egyptians. When Horemheb became pharaoh, he felt the need to return Egypt to its former glory. First, he eliminated the names of Akhenaten and that ruler's three immediate successors from all king lists and monuments. Therefore, official records began to show Horemheb as the pharaoh who directly followed Amenhotep III, Akhenaten's father. Additionally, Horemheb tried to give the country a new start by building temples to renew national devotion to the traditional gods, which Akhenaten had rejected.

Because Horemheb had no son, upon his death after nearly 30 years of rule, he gave the throne to his vizier, Paramessu, who was also a leading army general. Paramessu took the throne name Ramses I and was the first pharaoh of the 19th dynasty. Many of the pharaohs of that dynasty and the next, which turned out to be the New Kingdom's last family line of rulers, took the name Ramses. However, none were destined to achieve the formidable deeds and lasting fame of Ramses I's grandson, Ramses II.

Seti I

When Horemheb chose Ramses I to succeed him, the latter was at least in his 50s and died less than a year after becoming pharaoh, leaving the throne to his son, Seti I.

Seti was an ambitious ruler who, like Horemheb, wanted to reestablish Egypt's reputation as a leading world power. For his role models, Seti chose two famous pharaohs of the 18th dynasty—Thutmose III, best known as a great conqueror, and Amenhotep III, renowned for his building programs. Seeing himself as a spiritual heir of these rulers, Seti led armies into the eastern Mediterranean region. His official propaganda portrayed him as an invincible warrior who welcomed a fight with Egypt's enemies, who supposedly feared and fled before him. On a wall of one of the huge temples at Karnak, near Thebes, he ordered these words inscribed:

> He exults at beginning the battle, he delights to enter into it, his heart is gratified at the sight of blood. He lops off the heads of the dissidents. More than the day of rejoicing, he loves the moment of crushing [the foe]. His Majesty slays them at a stroke—he leaves them no heirs, and whoever escapes his hand is brought prisoner to Egypt.[36]

Although such propaganda exaggerated the extent of the pharaoh's real deeds, it appears that he did achieve considerable success in some of his campaigns. Seti captured several Mediterranean port cities, including Sidon, Tyre, and Byblos, which ensured that his country could keep getting the supplies it needed. Seti also fought the Hittites and their local allies in the region of Amurru, in southern Syria. At the time, Amurru and nearby Kadesh were subject to the Hittites, and the pharaoh wanted to drive that foreign foe out of what he viewed as Egypt's rightful imperial territory. It is unclear whether Seti's clashes with the Hittites were victorious; however, the pharaoh's propaganda makes it seem as if he scored great successes: "His majesty made a great slaughter ... smiting the Asiatics, beating down the Hittites, slaying their chiefs ... charging among them like a tongue of fire."[37] Most historians actually think these claims were designed to cover up Seti's failure to fully remove the Hittites from Syria.

The Battle of Kadesh

When Seti died, the Hittites were a bigger threat than ever to the stability of Egypt's empire. It was Seti's son, Ramses II, who finally faced off with the Hittites in one of ancient history's greatest battles. Ramses wasted little time in following up on his father's efforts. In the summer of the fourth year of his reign, the new pharaoh led an army to Amurru. No battle occurred, but Ramses seemed confident that this show of force would intimidate the Hittites.

This proved to be a miscalculation. The Hittite king, Muwatallis, challenged the Egyptian pharaoh to an all-out war over Syria. Ramses knew that he could not take this threat lightly. Not only was Muwatallis's army large, many of his soldiers were tough, seasoned warriors. Also, the Hittites possessed a huge and formidable chariot corps. Whereas Egyptian chariots were lightweight and carried two men, Hittite versions were wider, heavier, and carried a three-man crew. Also, the Egyptians used their chariots as platforms from which to shoot arrows from a distance, while the Hittite chariots were capable of shock tactics—headfirst charges into enemy lines.

Though the outcome of the Battle of Kadesh was a draw, Egyptians celebrated the heroism and strength of Ramses II, their leader who led them into war. Shown here is his chariot.

The test of the Hittite and Egyptian chariots came in the spring of 1274 BC. Ramses marched an army of about 20,000 foot soldiers and 2,000 chariots northward to Kadesh in southern Syria. Unbeknownst to the young pharaoh, Muwatallis had forces totaling about 40,000 soldiers and as many as 3,000 chariots. Ramses also mistakenly thought that the opposing army was camped many miles north of Kadesh and that taking the town would be relatively easy. Then, the pharaoh learned that Muwatallis and his forces were hiding on the far side of Kadesh, preparing to ambush the Egyptians. Quickly, Ramses tried to prepare his soldiers for the impending attack.

It was too late. A few miles to the south of the city, near the Orontes River, a large unit of Ramses's troops was surprised and crushed by the onrush of hundreds of Hittite chariots. Many Egyptians were killed, and the

The fighting at Kadesh had an impact on the history of not just Egypt, but also the entire region. This image shows Ramses II in action.

survivors fled to Ramses's camp, situated closer to Kadesh. Realizing that he had to act fast, the pharaoh sprang into action, as depicted in one of the official Egyptian accounts of the battle:

Taking up weapons and donning his armor, he was like [the god] Seth in the moment of his power. He mounted his [chariot, pulled by his prized horses named] "Victory in Thebes," and started out quickly ... His majesty was mighty, his heart stout, [and] one could not stand before him ... His Majesty charged into the force of the foe ... His majesty was like Seth, great-of-strength, like Sakhmet in the moment of her rage.[38]

For several hours the two armies fought, then, after agreeing to a temporary peace, the opposing kings returned to their countries and each claimed victory. However, in reality, there had been no clear winner at Kadesh. The Egyptians and Hittites maintained their uneasy standoff in Syria until about 15 years later, when each side returned to Kadesh and signed the first-known nonaggression pact. This turned out to be the end of an era for both nations. Not long afterward, the Hittites went into an irreversible decline and suddenly disappeared from history. The Kadesh campaign also marked the height of Egyptian power in the Near East. After the reign of Ramses II, Egypt's influence beyond its own borders steadily decreased.

THE BUILDING OF PI-RAMESSE

Archaeologists discovered this inscription dating from about 1272 BC, when Ramses II was building his new city, Pi-Ramesse. The words reveal how the pharaoh made a deal with the construction workers, agreeing to extend them certain benefits in exchange for their hard work:

You chosen workmen ... craftsmen in valuable stone, experienced in [working with] granite ... good fellows, tireless and vigilant at work all day, who execute their tasks with energy and ability! ... [I will give you] abundant provisions ... I am your constant provider. The supplies assigned for you are weightier than the work, in my desire to [generously] nourish and foster you! I know your labors to be eager and able, and that work is only a pleasure with a full stomach ... I have filled the stores for you with ... bread, meat, cakes ... sandals, clothing [and much more]. None of you need [to] pass the night moaning about poverty![1]

1. Quoted in K.A. Kitchen, *Pharaoh Triumphant: The Life and Times of Ramesses II*. Warminster, UK: American University in Cairo Press, 1982, p. 120.

Ramses's Achievements

In the remaining years of Ramses's reign following the great battle, the Egyptians could enjoy having a strong and constructive ruler with an enormous national treasury at his disposal. Ramses turned out to be the most prolific builder Egypt had ever seen. According to one scholar, Ramses "left behind a legacy of monuments unequalled by any other pharaoh of the New Kingdom. No site in Egypt was untouched by his builders and his monuments. His temples, chapels, statues, and [tablets] can be found throughout the country ... it is amazing how much building activity was carried out by this king."[39]

On the one hand, Ramses exerted considerable time and energy to the task of repairing or adding to older structures. At the great temple complex at Karnak, for example, he had more than 100 stone sphinxes carved to line the avenue linking the complex with the nearby Luxor Temple. Even more

Ramses II added more than 100 stone sphinxes to the avenue between Karnak and Luxor.

impressive were Ramses's additions to the gigantic hypostyle hall begun at Karnak by his grandfather. A common feature of Egyptian architecture, a hypostyle hall was a large courtyard covered by a roof held up by a forest of tall columns. Finally completed by Ramses, the hall had a total of 134 columns, 12 of which towered to a height of 70 feet (21 m), while the remaining 122 columns were 40 feet (12 m) tall. Covering the hall's walls were relief sculptures and inscriptions depicting Ramses' coronation and "victory" at Kadesh. Artistic renditions of the Kadesh campaign also covered the walls of the massive gateways the pharaoh added to the Luxor Temple. On each side of these gates stood a giant statue of Ramses.

Ramses also erected completely new structures all over Egypt, some of them enormous and impressive. Across the Nile from Luxor rose his main mortuary temple, which he named United-with-Thebes and historians call the Ramesseum. This was where the pharaoh's body lay in state after his death and where his chief priests prayed for his safe journey into the afterlife. Even more imposing was Ramses's great temple at Abu Simbel, on the Nile's west bank in northern Nubia. Carved from the face of a cliff overlooking the Nile, the temple's facade featured four colossal statues of the king sitting and staring out into the distance, as if surveying his vast domain. Three of these statues remain almost completely

VICTORY OVER THE SEA PEOPLES

R amses II was not the only pharaoh to have his heroics documented. Ramses III had carved on the walls of his mortuary temple at Medinat Habu the following, which bragged of his victory over the invaders now called the Sea Peoples:

> *Those who reached my boundary ... their heart and their soul are finished forever and ever. As for those who had assembled before them on the sea, the full flame [the fleet of Egyptian warships] was in their front, before the harbor-mouths, and a wall of metal [the Egyptian infantrymen] upon the shore surrounded them. They were dragged, overturned, and laid low upon the beach; slain and made [into] heaps from stern to bow of their galleys, while all their things were cast upon the water.*[1]

1. Quoted in J.H. Breasted, ed., *Ancient Records of Egypt, vol. 4*. New York, NY: Russell and Russell, 1962, p. 39.

intact today, and each statue stands 69 feet (21 m) high.

In addition to temples, giant statues, and other individual artifacts, Ramses constructed an entirely new city in a spot somewhat southeast of the Nile Delta. Called Pi-Ramesse, or "domain of Ramses," the city featured an immense royal

residential sector covering an estimated 4 square miles (10 sq km). There was a palace, a treasury, administrative offices, religious temples, army barracks, large-scale gardens, and a zoo. Outside the royal compound were shops for local merchants and the houses of the laborers who built and maintained the city.

The huge statues of the temple at Abu Simbel, shown here, remain largely intact today.

Decline of the New Kingdom

The many works and deeds of Ramses II were an inspiration to the Egyptian rulers who immediately followed him. However, none of them came close to his level of achievement. After he died, Egypt went into a period of steady decline. The last 5 pharaohs of the 19th dynasty, beginning with Ramses's son, Merneptah, had short, ineffectual reigns. The same was true of all but 1 of the 10 rulers of the 20th dynasty. In addition to weak leadership, Egypt fell prey to increasing pressures from the outside. Northern Africa grew steadily drier, which encouraged nomadic peoples dwelling in Libya, west of Egypt, to begin migrating into the Nile Valley. Also, Egypt gradually lost control of the eastern Mediterranean region, while the Nubian gold mines, long a source of wealth to the pharaohs, became less and less productive.

Even more troubling were attacks by foreigners from the north and northwest during the 12th and 13th centuries BC. Modern scholars collectively call these intruders the Sea Peoples. The largest assault by the Sea Peoples on Egypt took place in 1174 BC, the 8th year of the reign of the only strong and resourceful pharaoh of the 20th dynasty: Ramses III. He met and defeated a first wave of invaders in a large land battle in northern Egypt. Then, a second and larger wave of Sea Peoples struck. Its terrible onslaught was later depicted in a series of striking relief sculptures in Ramses's mortuary temple at Medinat Habu. These show how the Egyptians trapped the invaders' boats near the shore and fired massive amounts of arrows onto them, killing thousands. Egyptian soldiers also boarded the ships and fought hand-to-hand in a desperate attempt to save their country and way of life. These efforts paid off, as Ramses and his troops defeated the Sea Peoples once again.

The victory proved only a temporary relief during Egypt's ongoing decline, however. Some of the surviving Sea Peoples settled in the eastern Mediterranean region and took firm control, forcing out the few Egyptians left there. Egypt's long era of imperial power and influence was over, and in the centuries that followed, its inhabitants would find themselves struggling to survive in a land that was either divided and weak or ruled harshly by foreign-born kings.

THE END OF THE PHARAOHS

Following the New Kingdom were the two eras that historians call the Third Intermediate Period, which lasted from 1075 to 656 BC, and the Late Period, which lasted from 664 to 332 BC. Egypt was once again divided during the Third Intermediate Period. The North was ruled by the Tanite 21st dynasty, and the priests of Thebes ruled the South. While Egypt was divided between the Tanite dynasty and Theban priests, there is no evidence that there was conflict between the two regions. However, while there was no conflict, there was still steady decline, and this made it easier for foreign rulers to come in and take over Egypt.

Beginning of Foreign Rule

The first of these great foreign powers to attack and occupy Egypt during the chaotic Late Period was the Assyrian Empire, centered on the upper Euphrates River in Mesopotamia. In 671 BC, the Assyrians and their king, Esarhaddon, marched into northern Egypt and captured most of the region around Memphis in only a few weeks. In his royal records, Esarhaddon boasted,

> Without cessation I slew multitudes of his [the pharaoh Taharqo's] men … Memphis, his royal city, in half a day, with mines, tunnels, [and] assaults, I besieged, I captured … I burned with fire … His queen, his harem, his … sons and daughters, his property and his goods, his horses, his cattle, his sheep, in countless numbers, I carried off to Assyria.[40]

Esarhaddon was unable to subdue all of Egypt, however. Later, he launched a second attack on the country that was more successful, although some Egyptians stubbornly continued to resist occupation. In fact, the Egyptians staged several armed uprisings against various Assyrian kings.

However, in the long run, these frequent efforts to resist foreign rule were in vain. The truth was that Egyptian leaders at all levels no longer possessed the authority and resources required to create and maintain large armies. One viable alternative appeared to be hiring foreign mercenaries to fight for Egypt. For a while, Egyptian leaders used whatever funds they could scrape together to hire Greek soldiers, mostly from western Asia Minor. However, this policy ultimately proved unsuccessful. In the late sixth century BC, the Persian Empire, centered in Iran and Mesopotamia, conquered both Egypt and its main source of military recruits, Asia Minor. In 525 BC, the armies of King Cambyses, son of Cyrus II, founder of the Persian realm, swept into Egypt. This initiated the country's 27th, or Persian, Dynasty.

The Ptolemies

The Persians ruled Egypt with an iron fist. So when the Macedonian-Greek king Alexander III (later called Alexander the Great) marched his army into the Nile Valley in 332 BC, he was welcomed as a liberator. After establishing a new city, Alexandria, which he named for himself, Alexander departed and proceeded to bring the remainder of the Persian Empire to its knees. Egypt, however, was far from liberated, for he had left behind troops to control the country.

Moreover, even after Alexander's death in 323 BC at the age of 33, independence remained an elusive goal for the Egyptians. As Alexander's leading generals began fighting one another for control of his huge empire, one of these men, Ptolemy, seized control of Egypt. Not long afterward, Ptolemy founded a new dynasty—the Ptolemaic, or Greek, Dynasty, which lasted until 30 BC. Under the Ptolemies, Egypt became part of the greater Greek world that now encompassed the entire eastern Mediterranean sphere. To defend against other large Greek realms (such as the Seleucid and Macedonian kingdoms), the Ptolemaic government maintained a strong army and navy. However, over time, as Rome conquered the Greek states and the rest of the Mediterranean world, the Ptolemies became ineffectual, both militarily and politically.

In fact, Rome became the major foe and the ultimate undoing of the last of the Ptolemies—Cleopatra VII, daughter of King Ptolemy XII. She was also the last independent pharaoh of Egypt. Now seen as the most famous woman of the ancient world, Cleopatra was a highly intelligent, talented, and ambitious ruler who might well have restored Egypt to its former greatness. However, Rome was far too strong for any Egyptian or other Mediterranean leader to resist. Along with her Roman ally and lover, Marcus Antonius (Mark Antony), Cleopatra was defeated in a major naval battle at Actium, in western Greece, in 31 BC. The following year, she and Antony committed suicide,

Despite their legendary struggle, Antony and Cleopatra failed to fend off the Romans; their story has been adapted countless times throughout the centuries.

and Egypt then became a province of the Roman Empire.

The first Roman emperor, Augustus, summed up how most Romans felt about Egypt and its people: "Would we not utterly dishonour ourselves if, after surpassing all other nations in valour, we then meekly endured the insults of this rabble, the natives of Alexandria and of Egypt, for what more ignoble or more exact name could one give them?"[41]

Ongoing Discoveries— Thousands of Years Later

Thousands of years later, there is still much for archaeologists and historians to discover about ancient Egypt. Areas are still being excavated, and new ruins and new pyramids are still being found. In November 2016, 7,000-year-old ruins were found near the ancient capital city of Abydos, which would place the ruins in the first dynasty. "The researchers uncovered the foundations of huts, pieces of pottery and stone tools, as well as 15 large graves. The ruins may have been the final resting place for the capital's elites." Additionally, "the size of the graves discovered in the cemetery is larger in some instances than royal graves in Abydos dating back to the first dynasty, which proves the importance of the people buried there and their high social standing during this early era of ancient Egyptian history."[42] Given the age of the items and how close it is to royal tombs, researchers believe the ruins are from the very beginning of Egypt's history.

In April 2017, researchers found a 3,700-year-old pyramid dating back

CLEOPATRA

Although the famous Cleopatra VII was of Greek rather than Egyptian descent, she ruled Egypt as its last pharaoh. Some surviving evidence suggests that she was an efficient, practical, and thoughtful ruler who managed the economy well and treated her people justly. During her reign, no rebellions took place, and tax collection proceeded normally. In addition, she improved and expanded agriculture, producing large surpluses of grain and other foodstuffs, as well as replenished the national treasury. Cleopatra's taxation policies were fair by the standards of her immediate predecessors, who had grossly overtaxed the Egyptian population. The proof of her fairness appears in a surviving decree issued in 41 BC: "Nobody should demand of them [the farmers] anything above the essential Royal Dues [basic taxes]," it reads. "Nor shall any new tax be required of them. But when they have once paid the essential dues … they shall not be [asked] for anything further."[1]

1.   Quoted in Jack Lindsay, *Cleopatra*. London, UK: Constable and Company, 1970, pp. 127–128.

to Egypt's 13th dynasty. The pyramid was found 20 miles (32 km) south of Cairo, and the "remains consist of its inner structures, including a corridor that leads to a lobby that comes from ground level and up to a ramp on one side, and interior walls and columns covered in hieroglyphics."[43]

In addition to new ruins being found by physically exploring Egypt and excavating ruins, there is also the potential of using technology to aid archaeologists in finding as much as they can in Egypt.

Egyptologist Sarah Parcak uses satellite imagery and maps to find forgotten sites from lost cultures. Parcak and her team have found "more than 3,000 ancient settlements, more than a dozen pyramids and over a thousand lost tombs, and uncovered the city grid of Tanis, of *Raiders of the Lost Ark* fame."[44] These recent discoveries prove that even with all that has been found out about ancient Egypt, there is still so much to learn in the future, especially with advances in technology to aid in the process.

Notes

Introduction:
Opposing Viewpoints of Ancient Egypt

1. Herodotus, *The Histories*, trans. Robin Waterfield. Oxford, UK: Oxford University Press, 1998, pp. 108–109.

2. Plutarch, *Isis and Osiris,* in *Plutarch's Moralia*, vol. 5, trans. Frank C. Babbitt. Cambridge, MA: Harvard University Press, 1962, pp. 167–169.

3. Lionel Casson, *Ancient Egypt*. New York, NY: TIME-LIFE, 1977, p. 16.

Chapter One:
Egypt's Beginnings

4. Herodotus, *Histories*, p. 131.

5. Rosalie David, *Handbook to Life in Ancient Egypt*. New York, NY: Facts On File, 1998, p. 19.

6. Charles Freeman, *Egypt, Greece, and Rome: Civilizations of the Ancient Mediterranean*. New York, NY: Oxford University Press, 2004, p. 18.

7. David P. Silverman, "The Lord of the Two Lands," in *Ancient Egypt*, ed. David P. Silverman. New York, NY: Oxford University Press, 1997, p. 108.

Chapter Two:
Pyramid Building

8. "Pyramid of Khafre," *National Geographic*, accessed April 21, 2017. www.nationalgeographic.com/pyramids/khafre.html.

9. Herodotus, *Histories*, pp. 178–179.

10. Chester G. Starr, *A History of the Ancient World*. New York, NY: Oxford University Press, 1991, p. 59.

11. Quoted in "Who Built the Pyramids?," *NOVA*, February 4, 1997. www.pbs.org/wgbh/nova/ancient/who-built-the-pyramids.html.

12. Freeman, *Egypt, Greece, and Rome*, p. 25.

13. Quoted in James B. Pritchard, ed., *Ancient Near Eastern Texts Relating to the Old Testament*. Princeton, NJ: Princeton University Press, 1969, p. 228.

Chapter Three:
Reunification of Egypt

14. Quoted in Miriam Lichtheim, ed., *Ancient Egyptian Literature: A Book of Readings*, vol. 1. Berkeley, CA: University of California Press, 2006, p. 142.

15. Aidan Dodson, *Monarchs of the Nile*. Cairo, EG: American University in Cairo Press, 2000, p. 53.

16. Quoted in Lichtheim, *Ancient Egyptian Literature*, vol. 1, pp. 143–144.

17. Quoted in Lichtheim, *Ancient Egyptian Literature*, vol. 1, p. 136.

18. Quoted in Lichtheim, *Ancient Egyptian Literature*, vol. 1, p. 181.

19. Quoted in John L. Foster, trans., *Ancient Egyptian Literature*. Austin, TX: University of Texas Press, 2001, pp. 33–34.

20. Quoted in W.K. Simpson, ed., *The Literature of Ancient Egypt: An Anthology of Stories, Instructions, and Poetry*. New Haven, CT: Yale University Press, 1973, pp. 61–62.

Chapter Four:
The Creation of an Empire

21. Starr, *Ancient World*, p. 89.

22. Quoted in Lichtheim, *Ancient Egyptian Literature*, vol. 2, pp. 35–37.

23. Quoted in J.H. Breasted, ed., *Ancient Records of Egypt*, vol. 2. New York, NY: Russell and Russell, 1962, pp. 125–126.

24. Freeman, *Egypt, Greece, and Rome*, p. 35.

25. Quoted in Breasted, *Ancient Records*, vol. 2, p. 184.

Chapter Five:
The New Kingdom

26. Zahi Hawass, *Tutankhamun and the Golden Age of the Pharaohs*. Washington, DC: National Geographic, 2011, pp. 56–57.

27. Quoted in Lichtheim, *Ancient Egyptian Literature*, vol. 2, p. 172.

28. Quoted in Foster, *Ancient Egyptian Literature*, p. 35.

Chapter Six:
Religious Reform

29. Nicholas Reeves, *Akhenaten: Egypt's False Prophet*. London, UK: Thames and Hudson, 2001, p. 193.

30. Freeman, *Egypt, Greece, and Rome*, pp. 39–40.

31. Quoted in Lichtheim, *Ancient Egyptian Literature*, vol. 2, p. 91.

32. Lionel Casson, *Everyday Life in Ancient Egypt*. Baltimore, MD: Johns Hopkins University Press, 2001, p. 96.

33. Quoted in Ancient Egypt Online, "Amarna Letters," accessed July 3, 2017. www.ancientegyptonline.co.uk/amarnaletters.html.

34. Freeman, *Egypt, Greece, and Rome*, p. 40.

35. Reeves, *Akhenaten*, p. 174.

Chapter Seven:
Egypt's New Enemies

36. Quoted in John Ashton and David Down, *Unwrapping the Pharaohs: How Egyptian Archaeology Confirms the Biblical Timeline*. Green Forest, AR: Master Books, 2006, p. 166.

37. Quoted in Samuel Alfred Browne Mercer, ed., *Extra-Biblical Sources for Hebrew and Jewish History*. New York, NY: Longmans, Green, and Co, 1913, pp. 124–125.

38. Quoted in Lichtheim, *Ancient Egyptian Literature*, vol. 2, p. 62.

39. Zahi A. Hawass, *The Mysteries of Abu Simbel: Ramesses II and the Temples of the Rising Sun*. Cairo, EG: American University in Cairo Press, 2001, pp. 44, 48.

Epilogue:
The End of the Pharaohs

40. Quoted in Daniel D. Luckenbill, ed., *Ancient Records of Assyria and Babylonia*, vol. 2. New York, NY: Greenwood, 1968, p. 227.

41. Quoted in Cassius Dio, *Roman History: The Reign of Augustus*, trans. Ian Scott-Kilvert. New York, NY: Penguin, 1987, p. 53.

42. Danny Lewis, "Newly Uncovered Ruins Reveal 7,000-Year-Old City in Egypt," *Smithsonian*, November 30, 2016. www.smithsonianmag.com/smart-news/newly-uncovered-ruins-reveal-70000-year-old-city-in-egypt-180961235/.

43. Alexa Erickson, "Archaeologists Announce the Discovery of a 3,700 Year-Old Pyramid in Egypt," *Collective Evolution*, April 8, 2017. www.collective-evolution.com/2017/04/08/archaeologists-announce-the-discovery-of-a-3700-year-old-pyramid-in-egypt/.

44. Abigail Tucker, "Space Archaeologist Sarah Parcak Uses Satellites to Uncover Ancient Egyptian Ruins," *Smithsonian*, December 2016. www.smithsonianmag.com/innovation/space-archaeologist-sarah-parcak-winner-smithsonians-history-ingenuity-award-180961120/.

For More Information

Books

Brier, Bob, and Hoyt Hobbs. *Ancient Egypt: Everyday Life in the Land of the Nile*. New York, NY: Sterling, 2013.
   This book details the daily lives of ordinary citizens of Egypt and includes plenty of photos and maps throughout.

Cooney, Kara. *The Woman Who Would Be King: Hatshepsut's Rise to Power in Ancient Egypt*. New York, NY: Crown, 2015.
   This well-researched book focuses on the longest reigning woman pharaoh, Hatshepsut, and details her rise to and fall from power.

Freeman, Charles. *Egypt, Greece, and Rome: Civilizations of the Ancient Mediterranean*. New York, NY: Oxford University Press, 2004.
   This book by a popular historian contains in-depth information on Egyptian history.

Hawass, Zahi. *Tutankhamun and the Golden Age of the Pharaohs*. Washington, DC: National Geographic, 2011.
   This book features many photos of artifacts found in tombs and provides information on each artifact as well as detailed information on the Egyptians' way of life.

Lehner, Mark, and Zahi Hawass. *Giza and the Pyramids: The Definitive History*. Chicago, IL: University of Chicago Press, 2017.
   This book by leading Egyptologists has in-depth information on the pyramids, explaining their functions and including hundreds of photographs.

Websites

Ancient Egypt
(www.nationalgeographic.com.au/ancient-egypt/)
   This up-to-date, extensive website features numerous articles on ancient
   Egypt and photos of artifacts and the pyramids.

Egypt's Golden Empire
(www.pbs.org/empires/egypt/index.html)
   This extensive PBS website includes photos of art and hieroglyphics found
   in tombs, a timeline, and information on the New Kingdom, pharaohs,
   women in power, and Egyptian society.

Explore Ancient Egypt
(www.pbs.org/wgbh/nova/ancient/explore-ancient-egypt.html)
   This website has interactive photos of Egypt and its tombs and also has links
   to many articles on ancient Egypt.

National Geographic: **Egypt**
(travel.nationalgeographic.com/travel/countries/egypt-guide/)
   This website has a vast amount of information on Egypt's history and
   present and has plenty of photos, articles, and quizzes on
   ancient Egypt.

**"Space Archaeologist Sarah Parcak Uses Satellites to Uncover Ancient
Egyptian Ruins"**
(www.smithsonianmag.com/innovation/space-archaeologist-sarah-parcak-
winner-smithsonians-history-ingenuity-award-180961120/)
   This *Smithsonian* article and video details how technology is being used to
   discover ancient artifacts and ruins from lost cultures, including
   ancient Egypt.

Index

Picture Credits

Cover Nico Tondini/Photographer's Choice RF/Getty Images; pp. 6–7 (background) Gordana Adzieva/Shutterstock.com; pp. 6 (bottom), 27 (top) Vladimir Melnik/Shutterstock.com; p. 6 (top) Rogers Fund, 1930/The Metropolitan Museum of Art; p. 7 (top) DEA/A. DAGLI ORTI/De Agostini/Getty Images; p. 7 (bottom) Hulton Archive/Getty Images; p. 9 Gift of George F. Baker, 1891/The Metropolitan Museum of Art; p. 10 Orhan Cam/Shutterstock.com; p. 13 DEA/C. SAPPA/De Agostini/Getty Images; pp. 15, 32 bumihills/Shutterstock.com; p. 18 astudio/Shutterstock.com; p. 19 Jaroslav Moravcik/Shutterstock.com; p. 21 Mace-head of Scorpion King, 3100-3000 BC (limestone), Egyptian, Protodynastic Period (c.3200-3000 BC)/Ashmolean Museum, University of Oxford, UK/Bridgeman Images; pp. 22–23 Art Collection 2/Alamy Stock Photo; p. 27 (bottom) AmandaLewis/iStock/Thinkstock; p. 28 prill/iStock/Thinkstock; p. 30 Arthur R./Shutterstock.com; pp. 38, 43 DEA/G. SIOEN/De Agostini/Getty Images; p. 42 courtesy of the Brooklyn Museum; p. 48 CRIS BOURONCLE/AFP/Getty Images; p. 49 Anton_Ivanov/Shutterstock.com; p. 52 Kenneth Garrett/National Geographic/Getty Images; pp. 54–55 John_Walker/Shutterstock.com; p. 57 © iStockphoto.com/TerryJLawrence; p. 59 Hannes Magerstaedt/Getty Images; p. 60 XINHUA/Gamma-Rapho via Getty Images; p. 62 Jemal Countess/Getty Images; pp. 65, 69 DEA/S. VANNINI/De Agostini/Getty Images; p. 71 360b/Shutterstock.com; pp. 73 Rogers Fund, 1924/The Metropolitan Museum of Art; p. 75 Rogers Fund, 1950/The Metropolitan Museum of Art; p. 76 Everett Historical/Shutterstock.com; p. 77 Apic/Getty Images; p. 81 Christophel Fine Art/UIG via Getty Images; p. 82 mountainpix/Shutterstock.com; p. 84 Ewais/Shutterstock.com; pp. 86–87 Lisa S./Shutterstock.com; p. 87 Emanuele Mazzoni Photo/Shutterstock.com; p. 91 courtesy of the Library of Congress.

About the Author

Nicole Horning has written a number of books for children. She holds a bachelor's degree in English and a master's degree in education from D'Youville College in Buffalo, New York. She lives in Western New York with her cat and writes and reads in her free time.